Autism Runs Away

Book 2 of the School Daze Series

Dr. Sharon A. Mitchell

Copyright © 2016 Sharon A. Mitchell

All rights reserved.

ISBN-13: 978-0988055377
ISBN-10: 0988055376

OTHER BOOKS IN THE SERIES:

AUTISM GOES TO SCHOOL

AUTISM RUNS AWAY

AUTISM BELONGS

AUTISM TALKS & TALKS

AUTISM GROWS UP

AUTISM GOES TO SCHOOL WORKBOOK
(COMING IN 2017)

PREQUEL TO AUTISM GOES TO SCHOOL
(COMING IN 2017)

CONTENTS

Contents

Chapter 1 1

Chapter 2 10

Chapter 3 16

Chapter 4 23

Chapter 5 31

Chapter 6 35

Chapter 7 41

Chapter 8 44

Chapter 9 47

Chapter 10 50

Chapter 11 53

Chapter 12 61

Chapter 13 68

Chapter 14 75

Chapter 15 81

Chapter 16 85

Chapter 17 89

Chapter 18 96

Chapter 19 102

Chapter 20 109

Chapter 21 118

Chapter 22 121

Chapter 23 124

Chapter 24 128

ABOUT THE AUTHOR 129

OTHER BOOKS IN THE SERIES 130

Synopsis of Books in the School Daze Series 131

Autism Goes to School 131

Autism Belongs 133

Autism Talks and Talks 134

Autism Grows Up 135

Autism Goes to School Workbook 136

Connect with the Author 137

ACKNOWLEDGMENTS

I am blessed with the full M.E.A.L. deal editing team - Mary, Ellen, Andi & Lynn. Any errors are mine alone and exist despite their efforts. Thank you for your editorial as well as your copyediting skills.

This is a work of fiction, a figment of the author's imagination. Any resemblance to real people or events is coincidental. This story is for entertainment and information purposes only. The author assumes no responsibility for the strategies or suggestions described.

Chapter 1

Shrieks split the air. Ellie froze. She could make out the words, "No, no, no, no," but not much else. Then the screams came again.

Ellie hurried down the hall and broke into a run. The office, where was it? She should know this. Ben and Mel had told her to make sure to check in there before getting Kyle. Besides, she had no idea which room he was in.

The screams died down then rose to a new crescendo, accompanied by bangs and bumps, objects striking hard surfaces. Kyle!

The sign saying Office was just ahead. Ellie raced in and grabbed the counter. "Kyle. Kyle Wickens. I'm here to collect my nephew. Is he okay? Where is he?"

A placid gaze met hers as an older woman rose from behind a desk and approached the counter. "May I help you?" she asked.

Ellie gaped at her. "Help me?" What was with this woman? "Yes, you can help me. What's going on here? I want my nephew right now!"

The woman peered at her, the calm not leaving her face. "Have we met before?" she asked. "Your face looks familiar."

Was she dense? Or deaf? Couldn't she hear that ruckus down the hallway? Who cared about social niceties? Something was clearly wrong here. Some kids may be in danger, including her nephew. Couldn't this strange woman see that?

There was a commotion in the hall and Ellie retreated to the doorway, ready to snatch Kyle and run if need be. A group of small children lined up against one wall of the hall. With the door open, the yells and thumping were louder. The kids, however, did not seem perturbed, at least not nearly as perturbed as Ellie felt.

She turned her head back to the woman in the office. "What's going on?" she asked.

"I imagine they're doing a room clear."

"A what?"

"A room clear. That's what we call it when for safety's sake we bring the other children out of the classroom when one of their classmates is particularly upset."

"Upset? Upset! Is that what you call all this screaming?"

Before the woman could answer, Ellie spotted her nephew in the line of children. Her breath whooshed out and her shoulders came down from their hunched position. He was safe. She didn't know how she'd ever explain to her brother and sister-in-law if Kyle was hurt the very first time she was entrusted to pick him up from school.

"Kyle," she called. "Kyle, come here."

Kyle turned his head and stepped slightly out of line to see who was calling him. His face lit up when he saw her. "Auntie Ellie!" He waved and waved a grin on his face. "Hi, Auntie Ellie."

"Kyle, come here."

Kyle's grin faded and he didn't move other than to lower his hand.

"Get over here now." Ellie spoke more sharply than she'd intended.

Still Kyle's feet didn't move. But his hands, both of them now, rose. Instead of waving this time, his arms went out from his sides and his hands started to flap.

Oh, great, Ellie thought. Here it comes now. She spoke more softly this time. "Kyle, please come here now. We need to get out of here."

Kyle's eyes got wider. His hands flapped harder, and his gaze shifted from Ellie to the open doorway and back again.

A girl beside Kyle put her hands on Kyle's shoulders and pushed.

"Hey!" called Ellie as she stepped forward. Was this girl the source of the screams? Was she about to turn her attack on Kyle?

But, Kyle didn't look fearful and the girl was not screaming. She continued to push on Kyle's shoulders. As Ellie got closer she could see Kyle's arms lower and the flapping motions slowed. The little girl looked relaxed, but determined. As Kyle's hunched shoulders lowered and he took in then let out a big breath, the girl released his shoulders, turned away and began chatting to the girl in front of her.

Ellie took Kyle's face in her hands. "Are you okay?" she asked him.

"Hi, Aunt Ellie," he said as his arms went around her.

Ellie hugged him back. "Hiya, Munchkin. Are you all right?"

Kyle nodded.

"What are you doing in the hall?"

"Ethan got upset."

"Ethan?"

Kyle nodded. Well, that didn't tell her a lot.

"Let's go. Grab your things and let's get out of this place."

Kyle froze. She reached for his hand but he pulled back.

"What's wrong?"

Kyle stared at her. The boy behind him said, "We're supposed to stay right here."

"Yeah, well, I've come to get Kyle and I say we're leaving now."

"The rule is wait for the all clear," Kyle recited under his breath.

"What?"

The other boy explained. "After a room clear, we're supposed to wait here until we get the all clear."

A deeper voice behind her spoke up. "They're right, you know. When we've had to clear the room the other students are to wait against the wall until a teacher tells them it's all right to return to the room. The kids have not received their all clear yet, so Kyle is doing exactly what he's supposed to do."

"And who exactly are you?" Ellie's eyes blazed.

"His teacher."

"Oh."

He held out his hand. "My name is Rob Sells. And who are you?"

"I'm Ellie Wickens. Kyle's father is my brother. He and Mel are both out of town today and they asked me to pick up Kyle for them. I guess I'm a bit early but I didn't want to be late." Then she noticed the hand that was still outstretched. "Sorry," she apologized as she accepted his firm handshake.

"Ah, you're Mel's sister-in-law. She told us you'd be coming. Welcome to Madson School."

Was this place surreal or what? How could they stand here having a social conversation when just moments ago it had sounded like a child was being hacked to pieces in this very classroom?

"Is everything all right? What's been going on here?" she asked him.

"One of our students became a bit upset."

"A bit?

Mr. Sells flashed a grin. "Well, maybe more than a bit, but he's okay now. In fact, we were just about to go back into the classroom. Care to join us for a few minutes before it is home time?"

Without waiting for her answer, he turned to the children. "It's all clear now. Head back to your seats." The students turned toward the doorway and walked quietly into the room and to their desks.

Well, "desks" was using the term loosely. Ellie had never seen such a rag tag collection of furnishings in a school. Where were the desks of her childhood, those heavy wooden things with a seat attached to a side bar welded to the desk top?

Kyle was perched atop a grey plastic mushroom-looking thing. Its round top had a slight depression, which narrowed to a thinner stalk. On the bottom was another disk. As she watched, he squirmed. The poor kid had to wiggle to keep his balance because the stool or whatever it was, was warped. The bottom was not flat. Kyle didn't look perturbed, though. Kids could get used to anything, she thought.

Looking around the room, she could see other, similar stools, in different sizes. They were the lucky kids, she guessed. One poor kid didn't even have a stool; he was standing at a tall desk, a box of crayons out, his tongue protruding between his lips as he labored away at something.

A couple students sat not on chairs or stools at all but on balls. Looking closer, Ellie thought they looked a lot like the therapy balls she used at the gym, only smaller. Some seemed to have rubber protrusions on the bottom. Maybe to keep them from rolling away? A girl sat reading in a child-sized rocking chair.

There seemed to be an awful lot of movement in this classroom with kids rocking and wiggling and moving but there was surprisingly little noise. The kids had returned to the classroom and had taken up where they left off with their work. Even Kyle. Ellie was amazed at the calm in the room. Her heart rate was just starting to approach normal after the horrid screams that had come from this very room.

A voice spoke directly behind her. "So, what do you think?"

She just looked at Mr. Sells. She didn't know what to say.

"It's a bit much, isn't it, when you're not used to it. Today's classroom does not look like the ones we used when we were in school, does it?"

Ellie looked at Kyle's teacher. He was close to her age, possibly a bit older. He was pleasant-looking, with scuffed runners, cargo pants and a polo shirt. He did not look like any grade one teacher she remembered.

Without thinking, she said, "What are you doing teaching first grade?"

"I'm good at it."

"But don't usually women teach the elementary grades."

"Yeah. I actually trained for high school English, but needed a job as soon as college was out in April. The only teaching jobs open at that time of year were for substitute teachers. I spent a couple days in a high school then the next call I got was for an elementary school. I accepted, expecting to feel like a fish out of water. But, I loved it. And, the kids responded well to me. So, here I am."

She was sounding like her father who believed that only men should be in charge of businesses. She knew how much it galled her that her father didn't believe she could run the bakery simply because she was female. Now she was making the same sort of assumption about a guy who wanted to teach little kids.

"Sorry," she apologized. "It's just different. But, different is okay," she hurried to assure him.

Mr. Sells nodded, then moved to the front of the class. He circulated up and down the rows, checking work and exchanging comments with his students.

There was a light knock at the open door. A woman stood there, her brow furrowed, her shoulders sagging as if the weight of her hand bag was dragging her down. As Mr. Sells approached, her hushed voice asked, "Is Ethan here?"

"Hi, Mrs. Fellows. Come on in. He's right here, reading a book." He turned to Ellie. "Mrs. Fellows, this is Ms. Wickens, the aunt of one of our students. Ms. Wickens, this is Mrs. Fellows."

As the women said hello, a little head peaked out from the opening of a tent Ellie hadn't even noticed. It blended into a nook by the book shelves, a taupe kid-sized tent with the door flaps tied open. The floor of the tent held scattered pillows, some hand-sized soft balls, a couple bean bags and one small boy.

The child crawled out of the tent with a book in his extended hand. He gave the woman no hello, no hug or any other sign of recognition. The expression on his face did not change. But, he held the book out to her, immediately launching into a detailed explanation about the giant sawfly butterfly and how in its pupa stage, the caterpillar looked like bird poop. The woman tried to shush the child with a hand over his mouth and pressed him to her side, but he resisted and continued on with his spiel. The next page of the book covered buckeye butterfly, whose larva exactly matched the color of toadflax, its favorite meal. Ellie was impressed with the kid's knowledge, but the corners of his mother's mouth drooped. In fact, everything about her seemed to sag.

Ignoring what Ethan was saying, the woman looked to Mr. Sells. "He seems all right now," she said.

"Yes, he's calmed. The quiet of the tent helped settle him. We'll work on this some more tomorrow."

"Tomorrow? You mean he can come back tomorrow?"

Mr. Sells looked confused. "Didn't I understand that you had moved to our area and Ethan would be attending school here now?"

"Well, yes, but I thought that after this afternoon you might not want him back."

The teacher looked concerned. He gave her a warning look and knelt in front of Ethan. When he placed his hand covering the page of the book, the child's mother took in a sharp breath and tensed. Mr. Sells ignored that and continued.

"Ethan, it's time to go home now with your mom. But you'll be back tomorrow and we'll start a new day. I'm going to give your mother a copy of our visual calendar. Will you explain it to her? She's new to this so you'll have to help her. Please go get the copy off my desk."

As Ethan walked to his desk, Mr. Sells turned back to Mrs. Fellows. "This was your son's first day and new experiences are hard. It will get better each day.

"It will help if he has an idea of what he'll be doing during the day. Actually, that helps all of us, including you and I. Ah, here it is. Thanks, Ethan."

He spread the page on a nearby table and the three of them hunched over it. Mr. Sells explained that the pictures in this list represented the overview of the activities they would do the next morning. On the back of the page was the schedule of afternoon activities. Each picture depicted another subject or assignment. "Let's tell your mom what these pictures mean."

One by one he pointed to each line drawing and Ethan said the word associated with the picture. He only stumbled once, needing Mr. Sells help with the picture for music period. His teacher beamed at Ethan. "After only one day you already know these so well. Good job, Ethan." Again, Ethan's face didn't change in response to the praise, but he didn't look upset either.

"Why don't you show your mom where you hang your coat and you can get ready to go home."

Ethan and Mrs. Fellows were almost out of the door. "Wait," the teacher called. "We have a routine in this room." Mrs. Fellows stood hesitantly by the door; Ethan stood impassive.

Mr. Sells turned to the students. "Class, Ethan is leaving now. What do we say to him?"

Not quite in perfect unison, the kids said, "Good-bye, Ethan. See you tomorrow." The last tomorrows echoed.

Mrs. Fellows` eyes brimmed. Ethan turned to go through the door.

"Not so fast," his teacher said. "Wait. What do you say back to the class?"

His mom put a hand on her son's shoulder and tried to hustle him into the hall. "Oh, that's all right. You know what he means. Thanks for the sentiment and all."

Mr. Sells stood firm. "No. We have rules here. No student leaves for the day without saying good-bye." He stood waiting, his gaze locked on Ethan's. "Ethan, the class said good-bye to you. Now, what do you say?"

"But he doesn't talk much. You know what he means. We need to get going."

Mr. Sells was unmoved. His eyes never left Ethan's face other than to give Mrs. Fellows one warning glance. He looked like he could wait there all day. The class waited calmly as well. Only Mrs. Fellows looked uneasy. And Ellie. Ellie definitely did not want a repeat of that god-awful caterwauling

Ethan had produced earlier. How could this teacher risk starting that up all over again?

As everyone waited and his mom squirmed, a small word came from Ethan's mouth. "Bye."

His teacher beamed as if Ethan had delivered the valedictory address. He waved. "See you tomorrow."

From Kyle's seat a voice said, "See you soon raccoon."

Ethan turned his back as he said, "After a while crocodile." Then they were gone.

Ellie let out her breath. "Well, that was risky. What would you have done if he'd started screaming again?"

Mr. Sells shrugged. "I don't know. Wait it out, I suppose, like we did the last time. He left to continue his walk up and down the rows of students. Despite the strange seating, the kids worked well, most on their own, some conferring with neighbors.

Ellie thought about what the teacher had said. Wait it out. She shook her head. She knew how things could go, having witnessed some of Kyle's upsets.

When the teacher's path took him back to where she was standing, Ellie asked, "Don't you worry about impressionable young children seeing such things? God, I'd do anything to prevent Kyle from having one of these upsets."

"Is that good for Kyle?"

Ellie didn't know what to say. "He's my nephew. I love him. I can't stand to see him upset."

"I'm glad he has you for a champion but are you doing him any favors if you tiptoe around him? Look. Life is full of challenges and frustrations. Part of growing up is in learning how to handle them and how to handle ourselves."

"Yeah, but you don't get it. Kyle's just a kid and he's different. He has autism - an official diagnosis and everything."

"Yes, I understand that. But, so what?"

"So what? Autistic kids are different. They don't get the sorts of stuff that come naturally to other people."

"Yes, all true. But what are you doing to help him?"

"I try to keep his life as calm as possible. Have you ever seen Kyle in a meltdown?"

"As a matter of fact, I have," his teacher admitted.

"And what did you do?"

"I waited it out. Then when he was calm we went over what happened, what his choices would be the next time and what was expected of him."

"Yeah, right. You make it sound so simple. I'm ready to crawl into bed and put the covers over my head when one of these are over. Or have a good stiff drink," said Ellie.

"I can't say that I've never felt the same way but that wouldn't help the kids."

"Maybe not, but it would help me," muttered Ellie.

"I admit that watching a meltdown came be draining."

"No shit, Sherlock," came out of Ellie's mouth before she could stop it. She put up a hand, too late, to cover her face. Her fingers partially obscured her eyes so she missed the grin the teacher turned away to hide.

She was rescued by a chime that sounded from the hallway. In a minute she could hear the sound of children's voices and the movement of many sneakered feet. She looked at her watch and saw that school was over for the day.

"Sorry. Looks like I'd better get out of the way before I get trampled." She remembered the end-of-the-day mass exodus from her own childhood.

"There is no trampling in my classroom. Watch. You'll see. We have a routine for everything."

To the class he said, "Time to get ready to go home. Jenny, please bring up on the SMART Board the picture that shows what our desk should look like at the end of the day."

A little girl rose from her seat and went to the screen at the front of the room. She looked at the little pictures on the bottom, then put her finger on the one she wanted. The screen filled with a picture of an organized desk, pencils in the slot at the front, books neatly stacked along the side, crayons, scissors and glue in their plastic container. The kids busied themselves at their desks, some glancing often at the picture on the board, others tidying up without that visual reminder.

Mr. Sells gave the next instruction. "Put your hand up when your desk matches the picture on the board."

The teacher checked each child's desk with an approving word or smile, then had them get their things from their cubicles at the back. Each child lined up with their jackets on, their back packs over their shoulders. Ellie watched as each child approached the back of the line, with one arm held in front of them. When he was an arm's length from the child in front, he lowered that arm and crossed his arms in front of his chest. The teacher waited at the door, saying to each child, "Tell me in one sentence something you learned today?" After each response, he asked "Handshake or high five?" After Kyle's turn, he waited just outside the door with Ellie.

When the last handshake or high five had been exchanged, Ellie asked Mr. Sells, "What was that all about? I thought it was supposed to be a hug, handshake or high five?"

He grinned at her. "Maybe it's part of that gender thing you were referring to earlier. I don't like it, but it's probably better for me career-wise to keep some physical distance from my kids. A couple students in the room have witnessed spousal abuse and have not always had positive associations with men. Plus, some of these kids, like those with autism, need years to get used to certain rules. I'm safe and it would be okay to give me a hug but not all children have a sense of stranger danger and would over-generalize, thinking it's all right to hug any man. It's a sad comment on my gender, but that would not be a safe habit to get into. It was different in kindergarten but now they're a whole year older and we're working on behaviors that will carry them through the next years. We practice high fives or handshakes because that's a cultural norm they need to get used to."

"There's more to all this than meets the eye," Ellie said, but she was thinking that there was actually more to this guy than met the eye. Interesting. She'd ask Mel about him.

Chapter 2

No matter how many times she made them, cream puffs were still Ellie's favorite. Who couldn't love the fresh whipped cream oozing out the middle of the rich, golden puffed pastry? Then the sprinkling of powdered sugar with just a hint of cinnamon was the crowning glory.

Basted on top of that were the smells of Jeff's cooking. Corned beef and herbed chickens roasted in the oven, ready for their part in his deli lunch creations. Yes, the bakery had taken off since Jeff joined the crew, taking them from a struggling neighborhood bakery to a full-fledged bistro. Baristas no longer quit weekly because Jeff was able to keep the coffee equipment functioning. Plus, the extra revenue allowed Ellie to purchase needed upgrades.

Best of all was her dad. Although he would never admit out loud that Ellie now ran the family bakery, he'd stopped interfering, giving conflicting directions to staff, mixing up orders and all the other things that used to contribute to the business running in the red.

Oh, there were still problems. Having an employee with Asperger's Syndrome was new to her, especially an employee who had never held down a regular job before in all of his thirty years. But he was talented, oh so skilled on many fronts. They were learning to work together and once they'd hammered out the ground rules, a combination of flexible rigidity, if you could believe it, they rolled along with less conflict than she'd had with previous employees.

Jeff was not a morning person. Well, neither was Ellie, but it came with the territory of running a bakery so she just got used to it. She was also used to working alone in the early morning, relishing the peace and solitude as she prepared for the day's baking.

There was no need for Jeff to arrive as early as she, but he did need to get there in time to start the meat roasting to create his tantalizing deli sandwiches. Theirs was not a large kitchen and Ellie needed all the ovens for the baking first thing in the morning.

Initially, Jeff arrived when he wished and proceeded to commandeer the ovens for his meats. He seemed oblivious to the fact that Ellie had loaves rising, soon ready for the oven. Jeff was honestly perplexed when Ellie was perturbed to find her oven racks taken up with beef and chicken and pork. Jeff replied, "But I thought you wanted fresh deli sandwiches. How can they be fresh if I don't roast the meat before lunch?"

When Ellie countered with, "How can you make fresh deli sandwiches if I can't bake the bread?" Jeff saw her point.

Now, they had a system. By coming in just thirty minutes earlier, half of Ellie's baking was finished before Jeff's meat was seasoned, prepared and ready for the ovens. The temperature gauge of oven A was set at 350° and oven B was at 400°. Neither temperature suited Ellie nor Jeff perfectly but they each had to deal with it, adjusting recipes accordingly. The middle two racks in each oven were reserved for Ellie and Jeff could have the rest. He also got full oven use once Ellie's bread finished baking. Those were the rules. When Ellie overstepped them, Jeff let her know, even when that meant she had to get up an hour earlier to bake the Easter breads. Rules were rules. Besides, how could El complain when Jeff's cooking brought in so much extra business?

The tinkle of the bell signaled the arrival of another customer. Ellie didn't look up; her staff would take care of the orders.

When she'd finished icing the last of the donuts and arranging the cheese cakes in the display case, Ellie took a breather. She noticed the brimming coffee pots, telling her that someone had made new batches and customers would be ready for refills. She took a pot of decaf in one hand and Arabic dark in the other and made her rounds to the tables.

A lone woman who was glued to her phone caught Ellie's attention. The woman would scroll through her screen, read, and set the phone down, only to pick it up again moments later. Compulsive smart phone use was nothing new with her customers, but usually people looked more content, especially when wooed by the bakery concoctions and smooth, dark roast coffee. Besides, this woman looked familiar.

She was not one of their regulars. Ellie puzzled over where she might have seen her before. Stopping in front of the table with pots in hand, it came to her. Ethan's mother. Ellie recognized that look, the walking on egg shells, waiting for the next bomb to fall look this woman had worn when she picked up her son from Kyle's class last week.

Ellie had a few minutes. The customers seemed happy, her staff productively occupied. She asked, "Mind if I join you for a couple minutes? I could use a cup of coffee myself." Before the woman had time to formulate her refusal, Ellie left for a mug of her own.

"Hi," she said upon returning. "We never did meet officially, but I saw you the other day. I was at the school picking up my nephew and you were there for your son." She held out her hand, "I'm Ellie Wickens, aunt to a grade one Munchkin and owner of this bakery."

The woman's social skills forced her to accept the handshake even though her shoulders partly turned away from Ellie and her eyes made contact only fleetingly.

"I'm Sara Fellows. Mother to a grade one boy."

"Pleased to meet you. Is this your first time to our bakery?"

"Yes. We're new to this area." There was a pause. Ellie just waited. Sara continued, "You have a nice place here. This cranberry walnut bran muffin is wonderful."

"Wait until you taste our deli sandwiches."

"Oh, I don't think I'll be here that long. I'll probably have to head to the school any minute now."

Ellie turned her head to the side. "Why? Is this a short day, teachers' meetings or something?"

"No, nothing like that. It's just that I'm on call in case I need to go get Ethan."

"Why?"

"Why what?"

"Well, my brother and sister-in-law have a kid in school and I guess they're always on call like any parent. I think the school would be good about phoning parents if their child has an accident or something. But Ben and Mel don't act like they're on call all day long."

"It's different for us." Her eyes welled with tears. "Our son has autism."

"So does my nephew."

Sara gaped at her. Ellie nodded, confirming that yes, Sara had heard correctly.

"And he's in Ethan's class?"

"Yep. This is his second year at Madson School and he's in first grade now."

"I didn't know. I never noticed."

Ellie laughed. "Well, Kyle doesn't exactly have a big A painted on his forehead."

Sara's cheeks tinged with red. "No, I didn't mean that. It's just that whenever I've been to the school, I've never seen any other student in the room act like Ethan."

"What do you mean, act like Ethan?"

Sara's face changed. "Oh, god. It's just dreadful. He has these terrible meltdowns."

"Tell me about it. I've seen a few of Kyle's, even though they're happening less and less now."

"Less often? I think Ethan's have gotten worse over the last years." Then, it all came out in a rush. "Our lives are awful, just awful. Every waking minute is ruled by either Ethan's tantrum or the threat of a tantrum or doing everything in our power to prevent the next one.

"I can't work anymore. I got called to pick him up so many times when he was in kindergarten that I lost my job. This fall, it was even worse in grade one. The school didn't know what to do with him. He kept pitching these fits, throwing things, screaming and creating so many disturbances that the other kids couldn't work. They were afraid that he was going to hurt someone and he almost did several times.

"We moved to try a new school. Maybe a fresh start. Maybe a place where they don't know his past, maybe new kids who aren't afraid of him would help. But, it's started again, the same thing all over again and I don't know what we're going to do."

Ellie handed Sara more napkins to mop up her tears.

"I don't know a lot about this autism stuff and even less about teaching. But, I've seen my nephew make great strides since he's been at this school. It's not perfect, don't let me mislead you, but it's actually better and better. Part of it is that my brother has learned more about parenting in general and especially about parenting a kid with autism. It's not rocket science if even *he* can learn." She grinned. "It helps that he married Kyle's old teacher. Mel has her Master's degree specializing in autism."

Sara hung on her every word.

"I've only met Kyle's grade one teacher, Mr. Sells, once, but Mel thinks highly of him."

"He seems to stay calm and at least he's not furious with me and with Ethan, or at least not when I've been there." Sara's voice showed hope that her face dared not acknowledge.

Ellie studied her, and then decided to be frank. "I think I might have heard one of Ethan's meltdowns. I was there to pick up Kyle when his parents couldn't. I arrived early and heard the screeches."

Sara winced.

"I admit, they unnerved me," said Ellie. "But I seemed to be the only one upset, well apart from Ethan. The other kids waited in the hallway then went back into the classroom when Mr. Sells told them to. They got right back to work. *I* was still vibrating but everyone else seemed to take it in stride."

Sara tried to apologize. "I'm so sorry you had to witness that and sorry that he disturbed the class and even sorrier that this happens to my son. We try, honestly, we really do. We love our son. We're not bad parents, at least we try not to be, but we really must be if our kid acts like this."

"Hmmm. Most of what I know about this, I've learned from my sister-in-law. I don't think she holds with that bad parent theory or even a bad teacher theory. She explained to me that many kids with autism are just wired differently."

Sara brow furrowed like she'd never heard this before. "What do you mean?" she asked.

"Okay. I can't do this nearly as well as Mel does, but I'll give it a try. You should meet her someday, by the way. You'd like Mel.

"Kids with autism can be hyper-sensitive to some things, things the rest of us would hardly notice or dismiss them if we did notice. Like a thread from your sock lying across your toe. Or the swishing sound of rain pants or the hum of fluorescent light."

"I didn't know lights made any noise."

"I think it's just fluorescents," Ellie explained.

"Yes, they sure do," came from across the room. Jeff.

"Who's that?" Sara asked. "Was he talking to us? How did he know what we're talking about?"

"That's Jeff. He's in charge of the deli part of the bakery and our chief fixer-upper when anything breaks down. Oh, you should taste his sandwiches. You'll have to bring your family here for lunch someday."

"We don't really go out much and certainly, we can't bring Ethan to eat in public."

"Why not?"

"You never know what might set him off and how he might act."

Ellie raised an eyebrow as she looked at Sara. "This is a pretty casual place and you're welcome anytime."

"Thanks, but I can't see us chancing it anytime soon. A lot would have to change before we could eat out as a family."

Jeff's back was to them, but they could hear him add, "You just have to look at the situation from the kid's point of view."

Sara turned to look at Jeff's back. "How does he do that? He's on the other side of the room. How does he know what we're talking about?"

"That's Jeff." Ellie's smile took in both Sara and Jeff. "He's a man of many talents beyond sandwich making. He has hearing like you'd never believe. It may look like he's not paying attention but he's probably aware of everything going on in this building."

"You bet your sweet patootie I am," said Jeff.

"Jeff! That's probably not appropriate to say in a place of business."

"Probably?" he echoed. "Well, is it or isn't it? Make up your mind. And, not everything is meant literally. Didn't anybody ever tell you that? It's like an idiom. Besides, maybe you're patootie's not sweet. I have no personal experience with it."

"Can it, Jeff." Ellie laughed; Sara looked shocked. "Did I happen to mention that Jeff is my sister-in-law's brother?"

"Oh, so you know each other well. He's not just your employee."

"No, we're friends and relatives of a sort." Ellie continued. "And, did I also mention that he has autism?"

From Jeff, "Get it right, El. For those purists among us, my diagnosis is Asperger's Syndrome, still within the autism spectrum, but a subset characterized by no lag in communication, cognitive or self-help skills. Should I go on?"

"Not right now, Jeff, but thanks for offering. I think we've overwhelmed Sara enough."

"Okay. I know what it's like to feel overwhelmed." Jeff retreated to the kitchen to remove the corned beef from the oven.

Sara leaned forward and lowered her voice. "What's he doing working here if he has autism?" she asked.

A voice from the back yelled, "I heard that. Want me to answer it, El?"

"No. Thanks, but I think I've got it," answered Ellie.

Sara was mortified. "God, I'm sorry. I didn't think he could hear me from the back room. What must he think of me?"

There was no reply from Jeff.

Sara waited a minute. "Do you think my son could ever be like Jeff? Have a job? Be around people?"

"That's me. Role model to the masses or at least the masses with autism," came from the kitchen.

Ellie raised her voice to be sure it would carry to the kitchen. "Are you sure you'd *want* your kid to be like Jeff?"

"Yep, as soon as she tastes my corned beef on rye she'll be sure," Jeff yelled back.

Chapter 3

Mel looked up at the knock on her open classroom door. "Ellie, hi. What brings you here?"

"Hey Mel. I wanted to talk to you about something and thought this would be a quiet place without the interruptions of the Munchkin."

"He does demand your attention whenever you're around. He thinks a lot of his Auntie El. Come on in. Let me introduce you to Lori Nabaku. Lori's the EA, Educational Associate, in our room. Lori, this is my sister-in-law Ellie Wickens."

Mel continued. "And, I'd like you to meet Kyle's teacher, Rob Sells."

Rob nodded and Ellie said, "Good. I'm glad you're here. You're part of what I wanted to talk to Mel about."

"This sounds interesting," Mel said. Rob's expression went from open to guarded.

He turned to Mel. "You know I can't talk about Kyle to anyone other than you or Ben without written consent."

"It's not Kyle I want to talk about. It's Ethan."

"Whoa. That's even worse. If it was about Kyle at least I could have obtained verbal consent from his step-mother. But I definitely cannot and will not discuss someone else's kid with you or in front of you."

"I get that," Ellie said. "So what if I talk in generalities about how you're handling things in your classroom?"

The book she was holding rose to cover the lower half of Mel's face as she stifled a laugh. Lori's twitter escaped, before she said, "Guess that's my cue to get out of here before the fireworks start. See ya. Mel, at least you have that desk to take cover behind." With that, she was gone.

Rob looked like part of him wanted to be gone too, but the rest of him wanted to put this annoying, intrusive woman in her place. His initial thoughts of Ellie had been that she was smart, attractive, a bit mouthy but worth getting to know. Now, the first three still applied but he changed his mind about the last bit. Damned if he was going to run from her, though. He crossed his arms, leaned his shoulders back against the wall, bent one knee and rested the toe of his shoe against the wall. The picture of nonchalance, or so he hoped.

When Ellie didn't say anything he extended an index finger horizontally and waved it in a circular motion to signal her to go on.

"Thanks. Glad I have your permission." Ellie's tone dripped sarcasm. She turned to her sister-in-law. "Mel, I think this guy needs lessons on autism and on how to treat kids. I spoke with Ethan's mother."

That got Rob off the wall. "You what? How dare you seek out one my kid's parents? That's like stalking. What business is it of yours? How could you invade that family's privacy?"

"Keep your shorts on," Ellie reassured him. "I didn't seek anyone out. Sheesh. What do you think I am?" Then she added, "Don't answer that.

"Sara Fellows came into my bakery. I remembered seeing her with Ethan that day I came to pick up Kyle. You know, Mel, the day you and Ben were both away and Millie had that appointment?"

Mel nodded.

"Other people in the bakery might text and read messages on their phone but they don't cling to it the way Sara was. She couldn't relax but kept checking to see if she had a message. It was a slow morning and I had some time so I started talking with her. She told me that she couldn't stay long. She was waiting for a message from the school to come for Ethan. No, she didn't have an appointment and no, he wasn't sick. She was just used to the school calling her constantly to take her son home."

Ellie turned to Rob. "Did you know that she got fired from her job because she had to take so much time off work to get Ethan? The woman has no friends, no life and can't get one because she's constantly waiting for a call from the school. From *you*."

Rob started to speak but Ellie rushed on, giving him no chance.

"Have you no idea how to handle kids? If that's the problem, Mel here could help you. She's great with kids, especially kids with autism. She's taught us a lot - I mean my brother and my parents and me. We're all much better with Kyle than we used to be. Look, there are strategies you can use, things that really help."

"Like listening more and talking less," Mel said wryly.

"Well, yes. I don't remember the listening more but I did learn to talk less and show more, and all that whole visual stuff."

"Tell me more about this visual stuff you mentioned." Ellie missed the glint in Rob's eyes as he spoke, but Mel didn't.

Mel thought it was time to referee. "Look, Ellie. I think you mean well, but you don't know what you're talking about. You're way off base with Rob...."

"No," Rob interrupted, "let her speak. I'd like to hear what else she has to say. Who knows? Maybe I'll learn how to teach grade one from her."

"Rob," Mel started.

Ellie jumped in. "I'm not trying to tell you how to teach grade one. I'm sure you know more about that than I do."

"Well, thanks for that much anyway," Rob told her.

Ellie gave a half smile, the sarcasm going over her head.

"Look, I get that you can't have a kid screaming in your classroom. I heard Ethan that day. I don't know how anyone could stand that noise; the students certainly couldn't get any work done with that going on. And, it sounded like he was throwing things or beating something - that could be dangerous for the other kids.

"But it doesn't have to be like that. Mel could show you ways to get Ethan calmed down and ways to keep all this from happening. Just look at Kyle. He went from being one big tantrum to only having a couple a week and even these aren't such a big deal anymore."

"I'm happy to hear that Kyle and his family have benefited from Mel's wisdom," Rob told her.

Encouraged, Ellie nodded. "Sure, and you could, too."

Mel tried again to stop her. "Ellie, listen. You don't know what you're talking about..."

"But, I do. Don't be so modest, Mel. What you've done is miraculous. Without you Ben would still be floundering." She paused a second. "Hey, I don't mean that he married you just for the help with Kyle. I mean, well you know what I mean."

"Yeah, I get it. But you're not in possession of some facts."

Ellie turned back to Rob, earnestly trying to convince him.

"What I'm trying to say is that things can get better. If you'd just try some strategies, I'm sure Ethan will get calmer. Then his poor mother can get some peace.

"And what is school about anyway? Aren't kids here to learn? Maybe the stuff Ethan needs to learn first isn't written in the textbook on reading or math."

"Actually, the things he needs to learn all *are* in the curriculum in one form or another," Rob said.

"If he's ever going to learn, Ethan has to be in school and be in school consistently. Mel told us over and over to be consistent with Kyle. That means he has to be here every day like other kids."

She was not done. "And his mother deserves a break. She needs to know you can handle her kid and that he'll be in school every day. This might be her kid, but she needs a life, too."

She paused for breath.

Rob waited. "Are you done?" he asked.

Ellie nodded. "For now, anyway."

"I'll anxiously await your next installment. Do I get to say a few things now?"

Again, Ellie nodded.

"Do you have a child in grade one or soon to be in grade one?"

Ellie shook her head no.

"Good. Two points. One - my teaching methods are none of your business. I will and do explain my teaching to my students, their parents and to my principal. I don't need to explain myself or defend myself to you. Two - if you ever do decide to have a child, let me know before he or she is ready for grade one and I'll ask for a transfer out of here." He unfolded from his spot on the wall and headed out the door with a wave of his hand, adding, "Have a nice evening, Mel."

Ellie watched him leave then turned to Mel. "That wasn't much of a discussion, was it?"

"Are you talking about your diatribe to him or his parting comments?"

"The least I thought he'd do was defend himself. Or ask for your help," Ellie replied.

"El, just what did you hope to accomplish with this? You come in here knowing nothing about the situation, proceed to criticize a good man, accusing him of things you know nothing about."

"I do know about them. Sara Fellows told me all about what she's been through with the school and Ethan. She's a woman on the edge, hanging on by her toes. Her son needs help. She needs help, the kind of help you give people.

"I've seen what you did for Kyle and my brother; you turned their lives around and gave them a shot at normalcy. Ethan and his family deserve the same kind of help."

"How do you know they're not going to get it from Rob?" Mel asked.

"Well, it sure hasn't happened so far. That woman has been through hell with the school and her son. How many kids do you know who get kicked out of kindergarten? That happened to Ethan last year."

"Where did he go to school?"

"I'm not sure. She didn't say. But she did talk about his year and how she can't go anywhere or do anything because she just gets started and there's a call to come get him from school."

"And did she say who calls her?" Mel asked.

"No. No, she didn't. But it must be Rob or maybe he gets the school secretary to do it."

"Ellie, did anyone ever tell you that you should get your facts straight before launching into attack mode?"

"What? What? I wasn't in attack mode. Sheesh. I was just trying to help out, to point out to that teacher some things he might be missing. And, I did get my facts straight. I got them right from the kid's mother. How much more accurate can you get? You should have seen that woman. It's not everyday someone blubbers in my bakery."

"Sometimes when people are under stress they need to talk, sure. But their story might not come out in a coherent sequence. They may remember incidents and feelings they've had for a while."

Melanie continued. "Did it ever occur to you that some of what she said does not apply to Rob and this school? Didn't she mention that they had moved and were new to this area?"

Ellie paused. "Well, yes, she did but I thought she meant they were in a new house."

"They likely are, plus...."

"Plus what?" Mel didn't reply, just continued to look at Ellie. Then she got it. "Mel, are you saying that Ethan is new to *this* school?"

Mel nodded.

"How long has he been here?"

"The day you came for Kyle was Ethan's first day in Rob's grade one room."

"Oh, shit. And all those phones calls to come get him were not from this Rob guy but from their previous school?"

Mel nodded her head yes.

"But I saw her coming for Ethan. And I heard his tantrum just a bit before that. Surely the teacher must have called her."

"What were you doing when you saw her?"

"I was picking up your son, remember?"

Mel looked pointedly at her sister-in-law.

"Oh, double shit. I owe someone an apology, don't I? I have made a fool of myself, big time. He must think you have such an idiot for a sister-in-law and a loud-mouth one at that."

"Do you think he's still here? I'd better go apologize."

"Wait! You might want to let him cool off before...." It was too late. Ellie was out the door and down the hall. Mel shrugged and grinned. Ellie had met her match in Rob. She was sure they could both hold their own with each other. Each other - that thought flitted through her mind. Well, if there had ever been a glimmer of a chance for anything to develop between the two of them, Ellie had likely doused those flames well and good.

The door was closed but not latched and the lights were on. Peering through the door's window, Ellie could see Rob at his desk reading. She could only see part of the thin paperback he held in his hands, something about Journal... of Psychol.... Well, at least he was alone so she was not interrupting anything too crucial, as far as she could see.

She knocked.

Rob's head lifted and he looked out the window. He eyes met hers then his hand re-adjusted their grip on his book and his gaze returned to the page.

Hmm. Not very friendly, Ellie thought. But then, she may not have given him reason to feel warm and fuzzy towards her.

She rapped again.

"I'm working here and don't wish to be disturbed," he said to the door.

"I just want to apologize."

"Good for you, but I'm busy."

Ellie was getting annoyed. What was with this jerk? She was trying to apologize. Couldn't he cut her a break?

"Look. Can I come in? Just for a minute?" Was he going to make her speak through the door?

"Go away. School's out and I'm on my own time here."

Not exactly the chummy sort. "Mr. Sells, I'm sorry. I was out of line. I didn't have my facts straight and I blamed you for things that were not your fault."

He looked pointedly at her then back to his journal.

"Mel says you're a good guy and a great teacher. I'm sure she's right. It's just that I was so worried about Sara and her son. I was only trying to help. I've seen what Mel has done for Kyle and wanted stuff like that for Ethan's family. From what Mel's told me, I'm now sure that you do know how to teach Ethan."

"Well, thank you for that vote of confidence. Now, if you don't mind...."

"Can't you just open the door and we'll talk face to face? I'd like to apologize properly."

"Ms. Wickens, I've had a long day, I have work to do and frankly, you have nothing to say that would interest me. Please leave."

"But..."

Rob got up and walked to the door. Oh good thought Ellie. Finally. Now I can tell him how sorry I am and maybe we can even talk about autism things I've learned from Mel. Besides, Mel liked him and he really wasn't a bad-looking guy. They'd just gotten off on the wrong foot.

Then, he was in front of her. "Good-bye," he said. The door shut in her face and Rob returned to his desk, rearranging his chair so that his back was to the door.

Well. What a rude, arrogant man. The least he could have done is let her apologize. What a jerk! He was not worthy of her apology or her time.

Ellie stormed down the hall to tell Mel what Rob had just done. She stopped; Mel's lights were out and it looked like she'd gone home. Maybe that was just as well since Mel had not seemed too pleased with Ellie anyway.

Chapter 4

Sneakers squeaked along the floor, the swish of backpacks rubbing and squeal of little voices contributed to the excitement in the air. Milling little bodies heralded the arrival of another school day.

Mr. Sells greeted each child at the door. Some received a handshake, some a pat on the back, others a squeeze to the shoulder and others had a picture schedule placed in their hands. Rob Sells believed they all needed a personal touch to begin the day but how that touch should look varied depending on the current needs of each child. He strove to know his kids well and to give each what they needed to have a good day.

One head rose above all the others in the hallway. Mrs. Fellows. She approached the room holding on to the hand of Ethan. He was the only child to arrive at the classroom door with a parent and the only child whose hand was held by an adult. Well, they'd only been at the school a week and there was time to help Mrs. Fellows let go. But that would not happen until she was more relaxed and trusted Rob with her son.

He greeted Ethan with a, "Hey, bud. Nice to see you," and a raised hand ready for a high five. To his satisfaction, Ethan met his hand, even if his eyes did not glance his way. As always, Rob marveled at how this could happen, a kid accurately place his hand without his eyes obviously following the progress of the end of his arm. But, it happened. Rob himself was neither that skilled nor that coordinated and knew his high five would look more like a flail if he tried it that way. "

Once inside the room, Sara Fellows knelt to remove her son's backpack and jacket. Ethan stood impassive as she went to work. Rob sighed inwardly. Time to intervene.

"Mrs. Fellows, I have something to show you, some of Ethan's work that is quite good. Would you mind coming over here a minute? Ethan can hang his coat up himself."

"Yes, I'll be there but first I need to help Ethan." While her head was turned toward the teacher, Ethan had stepped away. His coat was mostly down his arms already and as they watched, he shook it off, picked it up and hung it on the hook marked "Ethan".

Sara gaped. "He never does that at home on his own."

"No? Well, you see now that he can, can't he?" Rob hoped the point was made and he could move on to other things.

"Have a seat over here, please." He handed her a strip of paper. "This is a copy of Ethan's visual schedule. It lets him know what we'll be doing during the day. I've found that it helps when the kids know, then there are no surprises for them. If you look you'll see that his schedule ends here at lunch time. That's *not* because that is the end of his day, but because just looking at the morning activities is enough at once. Just before lunch starts, he receives his new schedule which covers between noon and when it's time to go home.

"If you look around, you'll see that everyone here uses a schedule, but that they may look differently for different kids. We all share one big one on the wall over there," he pointed," then another one will appear on the SMART Board. For some of my students, that's all they need. For others, it's better to have a schedule of their own on their desk or attached to their book. If you look over there, you can see that Ethan has his on his desk.

"Some kids have visual schedules that cover the entire day, some for just a half day, like Ethan's and for some students even that is too long. Theirs is broken into four parts, separated by recesses and lunch."

He held the schedule strip out to Sara. "Here, this is your copy and the afternoon strip is on the back. It often helps if the parent goes over the next day's activities at home the night before or over breakfast in the morning before school. It won't take up a lot of your time. Ethan's starting to know our routine, so just point to each picture in turn and he'll tell you which subject the picture stands for." Rob beamed at her. "Can I count on you to help by going over this with Ethan at least once a day? I can assure you that it will help make your son's life easier at school."

Rob watched Sara's face carefully to judge her reaction. Was she ready for more? No, not quite yet. She still didn't look comfortable in the classroom which meant she didn't truly trust him enough with her son.

He invited Sara to sit and watch for a while.

"Why, is Ethan causing problems?"

"No. Oh, no, nothing like that. It's just that you're new to this school and I thought you might want to see how we operate in this room and how your son is fitting in. He *is* starting to fit in, you know."

"After the fuss he made last Friday, I wasn't sure you'd let him back."

Rob looked at her curiously. "Your son is a part of our class. Why wouldn't we have him back? He went through a rough spell that day, yes. But have you noticed that those incidents started to decrease as the week went on? Keep in mind that he's only been here just over one week and that's not much time to learn our ways. But, I can assure you that he will learn and he'll flourish here."

Sara looked like she didn't dare hope for that. "I'm really sorry that he's so much of a bother."

Rob stopped her there. "Stop. Your son is not a bother. He's a small child in a new situation. He's not sure of what's coming next or what's expected of him. His system is on high alert. It's my job, or rather *our* job together," his finger moved back and forth between himself and Sara," to help Ethan settle in and feel safe here. His mind won't be available for learning until he feels more secure. That's part of what that visual schedule is all about and why it's crucial for you to help by going over it at home daily with your little guy."

Sara's hands wrapped around the laminated strip. "I will, I will. Anything to help my son. He was so unhappy in his last school and they weren't happy with him. I just want him to fit in and be like a regular little boy." Then her face fell. "But I guess that won't ever happen. He has autism."

"Yes, he has autism. So do three other kids in this room. Can you tell which ones?"

Sara's eyebrows rose and her mouth formed a little oh. Even her shoulders seemed to sit up and take notice. "Really? You mean he's not the only kid with autism in this school? In this classroom? Which ones? Who? I can't tell."

"That's the point." Rob smiled at her. "You can't tell which students in this room have an autism spectrum disorder.

"Wait," Sara said. "Is it that one with the Educational Assistant beside him right now?" Even as she said those words, Lori Nabaku pressed her hand down on Kyle's shoulder then moved on to the girl ahead of him. She was making the rounds, speaking to each child and offering assistance where it was needed, not lingering long with any one student.

"What's she doing?" Sara asked.

"She's helping the students in the room."

"Isn't she assigned to just one child? If there are four kids with autism in this class, shouldn't there be four aides? What is Ethan going to do when he needs help? That's what I asked your principal that first day. Just who is going to help my son?"

"We are," was Rob's reply. "Mainly me - that's my job. Often Lori, Ms. Nabaku, is here and she circulates around the room with me. Between us, we get to all the kids. And, the kids help each other."

"But Ethan gets frustrated, he gets so frustrated. If he has a question or gets stuck you would not believe the meltdowns he has if someone isn't right there to help him."

"I know. We're working on that."

"But in the meantime, what's he going to do?"

"Pretty much what you're seeing him do right now."

As they watched, the little girl in front of Ethan turned with her paper and pencil in hand. She asked Ethan a question; he pointed to something on the girl's paper, said a few words and wrote something. The girl nodded, smiled, and turned back around.

Sara wasn't satisfied. "It doesn't look like she helped him at all. If I didn't know better, I'd say that Ethan helped her."

"Exactly," was Rob's reply. "Ethan's a competent kid. Sometimes he needs help; sometimes he gives help. That's our way in this classroom and in this school.

"Why don't you stay and watch for a bit? We'd love to have you."

"Oh, well, I have some errands to run and things I have to get done." Sara looked decidedly uncomfortable.

Rob studied her face a moment. "You know, I'm not asking you to stay so that you can help out or be responsible for Ethan. That's my job while he's here. You might like to watch to see how he's adjusting and to get to know our ways. Sit back and relax."

"Okay, I might be able to stay for just a little." Sara agreed to stay but she didn't comply with Rob's request to sit back and relax. She remained on the edge of her seat, her eyes on her son's back.

As the lesson progressed Rob watched Ethan's tension level rise. His shoulders were hunched. His feet swung faster beneath his chair. Time for some low level intervention.

Before he could move in, he saw Mrs. Fellows react. She got up from her chair to make her way to her son. Rob raised his hand in a stop gesture, wanting her to wait a few moments and to let him handle this. On the plus side, she seemed in tune with her son.

"Let's review a few of our strategies," he told the class. "Who is using their TheraBand® right now?" A few hands went up. "Let's all try it for a minute. Jerome, would you please explain to Mrs. Fellows what TheraBand® is?"

The child nearest to Sara's chair pointed to the Theraband, a thick, rubbery band tied between the front legs of every desk. He put his feet on it and pushed, relaxed, then pushed again several times. "See?" he asked Sara. "Sometimes I work better when I do this."

The rest of the class returned to their work, some pushing on their TheraBand. Rob noted that Ethan was trying this and his tension level decreased enough that he picked up his pencil. Still, his arousal level didn't seem quite regulated so he'd keep an eye on this student.

From the back counter, Rob snagged a weighted cushion, a square about a foot long, made of brown corduroy and filled with material that added weight. He approached Ethan's desk. "Here, bud. Want to give this a try? Put it here on your lap and tell me what you think. Some kids find that it feels good and they can concentrate on their work better when they use one. I'd like your opinion, please. I'll be back in a minute to hear what you think about it." Then he walked away.

With his head turned slightly in another direction, Rob observed Ethan. First Ethan ran his hands over the surface. Then he flipped the cushion over several times, rearranging it on his legs. Then he settled his butt more firmly into the back of his seat, picked up his pencil and went back to work.

It was time to change topics. Rob flicked the lights two times, the signal that he wanted the class's attention. "Let's take a look at our visual schedule." He brought the pictures up on the SMART Board. "Follow along on the board or on your own copy if you wish. Notice that we're just finishing math. Next on the list is circle time on the carpet. I'll start the time timer on the board and when the red color has all run out, I want you all in your places on the carpet." He started the timer and five minutes showed bright red in a gradually diminishing slice.

Some of the students put their books away and sat in their places on the carpet. Others first wrote a little more on their papers before putting that work in their basket. Ethan looked uncertain.

"Class, what do we do if we don't quite get finished some work?"

Several little voices said, "We put it in our red folder."

"What clue does the red folder give us?"

"To stop and look in here for any work we need to do."

"Right," Mr. Sells approved. "Anyone who is not finished, go put that paper in your red folder and there will be time to complete it later." He saw Ethan standing with his paper in hand, his eyes wide as he glanced around. Another student was close by who could help. "Doug, Ethan's new and hasn't used his red folder very often. Will you please show him where it is?"

"This way," Doug said to Ethan, who followed him to the shelf under the window.

Rob saw Sara's shoulders slump with relief. Likely she'd thought a meltdown was imminent. Well, so had he, but Ethan kept it in control. Good for him. Now for the hard part.

Although circle time had many benefits socially and academically, it could be a trying time for many kids. The opportunity to leave their desks and move to another area was a good thing. But sitting in close proximity to others on the floor could be tough for anyone sensitive to touch and also anyone who didn't have a good sense of where their body was in space.

Sitting in a circle looked deceptively simple. First it meant a change in activity and transition times were hard. Then each child had to sit near to his neighbor but without touching. Arms, legs and feet must be kept under control and out of other kids' spaces. There wasn't a lot of wiggle room when little bodies were seated close.

So, Rob had masking tape boxes drawn on the floor, one for each child. The ones in the outer ring were a little larger. Those were reserved for those children who needed even more spatial reminders. Two kids sat on child-sized rocking chairs, rockers with stops on the runners, preventing them from moving backward or forward too far. A couple of kids sat on plastic chairs with arm rests. One used a bean bag chair, the smaller one borrowed from the reading corner. Jerome brought along a weighted vest, knowing that would help him remain focused during their circle discussion. Several students sat on small, inflated cushions designed to allow some wiggle motion. Jerome picked up the lap weight Ethan had left behind on his chair. "Hey, Ethan," he asked. "May I borrow this?"

"Yeah," came the reply. Rob reminded the boys that there were more weighted products on the shelf if anyone wanted one.

As they started the lesson, Rob could see that Ethan was not comfortable. He wasn't the only one; Kyle was showing signs of anxiety as well. Best nip this in the bud before anyone became too upset. Especially with Mrs. Fellows sitting on the edge of her seat, ready to leap into action if Ethan looked on the verge of a tantrum.

"Before we go any further, Dr. Hitkins needs some help in the office. She needs some paper for the photocopier. Will a couple of you take her some, please?" Hands went up. "Kyle, would you carry two reams of paper and Ethan would you take two as well, please? Kyle, you'll need to show Ethan where we keep the paper and how to get to the office."

He turned to Jerome, seated nearest his desk. "Would you please give Kyle and Ethan each an iPod then bring one to me?" He had planned to stay in his seat in the circle, but could see Sara's growing tension. She'd left her chair and was headed to her son. Before Rob could get there, she had her hands on Ethan's shoulders, bracing him against her.

This might take a while, Rob thought. He signaled to Lori to take over circle time for him.

"Where are you sending my son," Sara asked. "He's new and he's only six. He doesn't know his way around this building. You can't ask him to leave the room, to run errands for you. Don't you have people who do that kind of thing for you?"

"It's fine and they'll be fine. The office is just down the hall and Kyle's been there before. He knows the way, don't you, Kyle?" Kyle didn't look as confident as Rob had hoped. But, that's what the iPods were for.

Rob took the three iPods from Jerome with a thank you, and draped the lanyard of one around his neck. He then held out one each to Kyle and Ethan. Kyle placed a lanyard around his neck and turned the iPod so the screen was facing out. Ethan watched Kyle, then copied.

This didn't make Sara feel any better. "What are you doing? These are only small boys. They can't handle expensive electronics like this. What if they break them? What if they drop them?"

"That's why we have them on lanyards so they don't get dropped. Watch. You'll see how we use them."

Turning to Kyle, Rob said, "Do you remember how we use FaceTime?"

Kyle pressed the Home button and soon Rob could see Kyle's grinning face on Rob's own iPod. "Good. Now show Ethan what you did to get into FaceTime."

Ethan, like most kids was a quick study and soon the boys were Face Timing each other, even though they were standing only arm's length apart.

"Now, Kyle, do you remember when to FaceTime me?"

"At the corner."

"Right. There's a table there where you can set down the paper while you FaceTime me to let me know where you are. Do you think we should let Ethan's mom in on this, too?" He handed her another iPod. She was hesitant, so he had Jerome show her how to start the FaceTime app.

"Okay. Kyle how many reams of paper should you each take?"

"Two."

"How many will you take to the office all together, between you?"

The boys conferred a minute but were able to come up with the number four.

"Show Ethan where the paper is, each of you pick up your two reams, then head to the office. Don't forget to FaceTime us when you get to the corner."

Sara was clearly still unsure about her son venturing into the bowels of the school without an adult. While the boys gathered their packaged paper stacks, Rob motioned Sara to the door. He pointed down the hallway so she could see the sign marked Office not too far away. Then he asked her to step back from the doorway. It wouldn't do the boys' confidence any good to see them hovering, unsure if the kids could carry out this task on their own.

As the boys left, carefully carrying their weighty loads of two reams each, Rob pulled the classroom door mostly closed. Sara started to protest but Rob cut her off. He flicked the intercom button quickly two times and explained that this was the sign to the school secretary to watch for students coming to the office with an errand. She would be watching for them and contact the teacher immediately if the kids didn't appear in a few minutes.

Before Rob could begin to explain to Sara the benefits of heavy work and the calming effects from carrying something heavy, there was Kyle's voice over FaceTime. Sara snatched up her iPod to see her son's grinning face. "How are you doing, little man?" she asked him.

Using his iPod, Kyle told his teacher that they had made it to the corner and were now going to the office to deliver the paper. Sara could see the tiny image of her son's face nodding in agreement to Kyle's message.

"I did it, mom!" were Ethan's first words when the boys returned to the classroom. Sara gazed at her son. Rob hoped she was seeing a different Ethan, a child capable of tackling new things and succeeding. Kyle gathered the iPods and put them away. He and Ethan rejoined the circle and sat calmly for the rest of the time.

Chapter 5

"Sara! What are you doing here?"

Oh, no, Rob thought he recognized that voice. Blast. What was that darned woman doing here? Again. And in his classroom no less.

Ellie continued without waiting for Sara's reply. "I was bringing my sister-in-law a sandwich for lunch when I noticed you as I walked by the room. Hey and there's Munchkin." Ellie's nephew, Kyle launched himself at her, evading the other kids who were getting their lunches out of their backpacks. "Hey, big guy. I brought your mom a yummy sandwich from the bakery. And, there's something special waiting for you at home."

Ellie turned warily to Rob. "Hi," she said. "Sorry to intrude."

He just bet she was sorry. Intrude seemed to be one of the things she did best. He crossed his arms. Sara looked between the two of them. Despite her pressing errands, she'd ended up staying the entire morning in the grade one room, looking more relaxed as the hours passed without major incidents.

When Rob didn't say anything, Ellie said, "All I ever seem to say to you now is sorry."

Rob waved his hand. He didn't want to talk about her being sorry or about anything else with this woman. "I'm sure Mel is eagerly awaiting her sandwich. Her room is just down the hall." He could not get her out of here fast enough. Something about her made him antsy.

Sara complied with a request for help opening a child's thermos and was soon busy with her son's classmates. Ellie stepped closer to Rob, rather than out the door as he would have preferred.

"Mr. Sells, I really am sorry, you know. I'd like to apologize properly."

Not now, not in front of his kids, in fact, not ever was Rob's preference.

"Look, let's just call it a day. We might bump into each other if you're visiting Mel or come for Kyle, but that's it. We can be civil to each other for those few minutes. Other than that we'll stay in opposite corners of the city if I have my way. Now, I need to see to my class."

Ellie couldn't see what urgently needed his attention in the classroom. All the kids were eating in their desks and chatting. "Here," she said. She reached into her back pocket and pulled out a slightly crumpled bakery coupon, good for one coffee and a muffin or dainty. She handed him the slip of paper. "At least accept this as my apology."

He couldn't very well refuse the paper when his students might be looking. He took it, muttered, "Thanks" and turned away.

Mel was quite an all right person, Rob thought. Her husband, Ben seemed okay and their son, Kyle, was a great kid. How did she ever end up with a sister-in-law like Ellie? They sat in the staff room after school chatting.

"How's your boys' group coming along?" asked Mel.

"Fine but some of the sports games we had planned aren't to everyone's liking. They need some physical activity but a bunch of these guys are more into computer gaming than soccer games. You can tell just by looking at a couple of them just how much time they must spend plastered in front of a screen.

"I know I'm not going to change that, but if I could channel their computer interest into something productive, we might be getting somewhere."

"What do you have in mind?" Mel asked.

"Well, in my ideal world, I'd teach them programming. Not that I know a lot about it but surely there are some kid-friendly programs out there that could help these guys create their own games. That might be a skill they could turn into a job one day, turn an obsession into an occupation or at least a skill that could lead to an occupation."

Warming to his subject, he continued. "And, if I somehow run into buckets of money, I'd like to take it further. I'd like to teach these kids how to refurbish computers or even better, to build computers from the ground up.

"I don't know a lot about this, but I think I could learn enough to get the kids started. They're so smart - if I give them just the basics I think they'd take it and run. Buying a new computer is prohibitive for many of their families but you know, I've heard of this other operating system that's free and there are lots of open source software options that would not cost a thing."

"That operating system you're talking about is probably a version of Linux. There are lots of Linux distros, most free but some cost just a bit to buy the disc. Some forms of Linux are pretty complex, others easier than Windows."

"How do you know all this? Did you used to teach computers?"

"Never. And I sound better than I actually am. The little I know I learned from my brother who can talk ad nauseum about all things computer related. He's a big fan of Linux distros and believes everyone should have that running their computers rather than Windows."

"Why?"

"He says that Linux is more stable, less prone to error messages, freezing up and that sort of thing. And, you get away from the worry about computer viruses and malicious software invading your machine. It's also free or nearly free as compared to hundreds of dollars for the common operating systems."

"But don't most programs run on Windows?"

"Yep, most do. But a lot of them will also run on many Linux distros."

"Distros?"

"Distributions. We think *we* use jargon in the education field but you haven't seen anything like the lingo techs and programmers use."

"Is Linux something kids could use?"

"Some versions, as far as I know. Jeff's told me that some forms of Linux are favored by programmers and are heavily command oriented, sort of like the old DOS computers. But some other Linux versions are no brainers that even I can use.

"In fact, my home machine runs on Linux. My old computer was gasping its last breath and Jeff offered to build me a new one for under $300. I didn't think it could be done, but this computer is faster and more powerful than any I've had before."

"What can you do on it if it runs on Linux?"

"I don't have huge computing needs. I'm not a gamer. I use it for researching on the Internet, emails, managing my music, accounting and word processing."

"So you can run Microsoft Word® on a Linux computer?"

"I'm not sure about that," Mel replied. "I've never tried. I use something similar, except that it's free. And, stuff I work on at home opens up in Microsoft on my work laptop and vice versa. Files convert just fine."

"Free?"

"Free. Like Microsoft Office®, Apache's Open Office® has a word processor, spread sheet, database, presentation maker and stuff like that."

"Free. Do you know how much I paid to have Office on my home computer?" Rob asked.

"Yep."

"How do I learn about all this stuff? Did you take a course? Do online stuff?"

"My brother. If you ask him, he'll tell you more than you ever possibly wanted to know. The problem will be in getting him to *stop* explaining."

"Do you think he'd be willing to talk to me? Maybe even help with my boys' group?"

"Talk to you, for sure. I'm positive. About the boys' group, well, you'll have to ask him. I don't know how good he is in front of groups but you never know. He loves sharing his interest with people."

"Is there a way I can contact this guy?"

"He's not big on keeping his phone on. But he hangs out at this bakery on 21st Street. Drop by there almost anytime and you'll find him puttering about."

"Do they have computers there?"

"Their Internet cafe part was pretty much just decoration until Jeff came along. Now those machines are in tip top shape."

Chapter 6

He stood outside and pulled the crumpled piece of paper from his back pocket. Yep, this was the same bakery that woman Ellie had given him the coupon for. He might as well make use of it. Even if he didn't like *her* he did like good coffee.

The bell jingled as Rob pushed open the door. A young woman behind the counter smiled and said, "Be right with you in a moment." The smells of sweet dough, cream and sugar mingled with roasted chicken and beef. Rob paused just to take in the aromas, getting sidetracked from his mission.

He perused the counter windows and placed his order. Then he asked, "Would you know if there's a guy named Jeff here?" He was pointed to a man prying the back off one of the computers along the wall. Ah, that fit with what Mel had told him about her brother.

"Hi. Are you by any chance Jeff?" he asked.

"Yes." The man replied but kept his back to Rob, intent on the bowels of the computer.

Rob tried again. "Ah, can I talk to you a minute?"

"Yes." Well, at least that was a reply but still no eye contact.

"Have I caught you at a bad time?"

"No."

Well, this wasn't going very well. Rob stood there, uncertain of what to do next.

Then Jeff spoke. "Are you shy?"

What? "No, not particularly," he replied.

"I thought you said you wanted to talk."

"I did. I mean I do, but you looked busy and I thought I was interrupting you."

"Oh, did I forget to make eye contact? Observe the social niceties?" He turned to face Rob and stuck his hand out. "Hi. I'm Jeff. How are you today?"

This was weirder and weirder but rather intriguing. "I'm Rob Sells. Mel suggested I come here to ask you some computer questions. I teach with your sister at Madson Elementary School."

Jeff's face widened into a grin. He thumped Rob on the shoulder with more force than Rob thought warranted. Rob studied Jeff's face, but he seemed open and delighted to see him now.

"Any time, any time. Any friend of Mel's can drop by anytime. And computers are my favorite subject. What do you want to know, or should I just talk about the most recent fascinating bits?"

"No, no." Rob held up his hand. It was dawning on him. Hadn't Mel once said something about her brother having autism? Now it made sense and he was more comfortable. "There are some specific things I want to know, if you've got a minute."

Rob explained about the boys' group he ran Friday evenings and how some of the kids were more interested in computers than sports. He wanted to steer them away from just playing games to maybe building games and to learning more about the inner workings of computers. But they were on a really tight budget so he needed to do things cheaply.

"You've come to the right place, my man. You might need a bit of cash, but we can do this thing on the cheapo, scrounging parts and picking the right distros."

"Do you think you could give us a hand? Steer me in the right direction?"

"Sure. When?"

"Well whenever it's convenient for you. I work during the week but this is Saturday and I'm free for the rest of the afternoon."

"Okay."

"Okay?"

Jeff nodded his head toward the door. "Let's go. I can show you some of the stuff at my place and you can see what you might be getting into."

As they started to rise, there was a grinding sound, a sound different than the one of grinding coffee beans. This one sounded metallic. There was a yell.

"Jeff, it's doing it again."

Jeff was already on his way over to the espresso machine. Soon it was apart, Jeff's hands in its innards, Rob forgotten. Rob sat down to finish his coffee, which was excellent, by the way. He hoped that when Jeff was done he'd remember their plans.

A woman whirled out from a doorway, put her hand on Jeff's shoulder, gave it a squeeze, and said, "Thanks. We don't know what we'd do without you." She returned to the back of the shop, without once looking into the customer area. Rob thought there might be something familiar about her, but it all happened so fast he didn't pay much attention. His gaze was fixed on the display case. While he waited he might as well sample another of the bakery's delectable offerings.

Rob was just wiping the last of the powdered sugar off his face and the front of his shirt when Jeff appeared in front of him. "Ready?" Jeff asked. He didn't wait for Rob's answer but headed for the door.

Rob scrambled to catch up. "Sorry," he said as he jostled a table, almost upsetting a woman's latte.

Jeff's hand was pushing open the door when a female voice said, "Where do you think you're going?"

The men turned and there she was. That blasted woman turned up everywhere, Rob thought. Ellie, Mel's sister-in-law. And, what was she wearing? All white might be in fashion but those baggy pants and stained, stiff, high collared cotton shirt certainly weren't the latest thing in haute couture. And why was her hair plastered to her head? Was that a net thingy over her hair? Ellie stood with her hands on her hips glaring at Jeff.

Rob looked at Jeff, who appeared unconcerned. Maybe this was normal mode for Ellie; she's certainly not been warm and fuzzy whenever Rob had seen her. Well, maybe that wasn't quite fair. Obviously her nephew adored her and Mel seemed fond of her. Maybe Rob and Ellie just rubbed each other the wrong way.

She repeated herself. "Where do you think you're going, Jeff?"

"Home. I gotta show this guy some stuff. He wants to teach kids to build these Linux boxes then design games."

"Now?"

"Yeah." What was her problem, Jeff wondered. Oh, now he remembered. "Sorry, Ellie. Are you feeling left out? That's not polite. I wasn't thinking of your feelings. Why don't you come with us? We'd like your company, wouldn't we, ah....?" He looked at Rob. "What did you say your name was?"

Rob and Ellie spoke at the same time.

"Rob. My name is Rob Sells and I teach with your sister."

"Now? Now? The bakery doesn't close for another half hour. Look around. We still have customers here."

Rob couldn't see what that had to do with either him or Jeff. But Ellie's get-up was starting to make sense. "You work here?" he asked her.

"Do I *work* here? Yeah, I'd say so. I'm here every morning by five and close the place up twelve hours later. I guess I do work here. In fact, I own the place."

Rob's head went up. He looked at Ellie and around at the obviously flourishing business. "Nice place you have here." Maybe there was more to this pesky woman than he'd thought at first. Then he remembered. "Oh, so that's why you had that coupon you gave me hanging around in your pocket. I thought you were just passing on to me something that had been given to you."

"You really don't think much of me, do you?"

This was not the time to get into it, Rob thought, not with customers around. Actually, not anytime. Avoiding each other would solve a lot of problems.

"So, are you coming or not?" asked Jeff. He was shifting his weight from one foot to the other.

"No and neither are you," Ellie started, but was interrupted by Rob.

This annoying woman was seriously interfering in his life and trying to run Mel's brother's life to boot. The guy obviously had time on his hands since he was just picking away at the computers when Rob walked in. "Why don't you cut the guy a break?" he asked Ellie. "He's just trying to give me a hand; Mel told me Jeff would likely be willing to help. And, geez, it's for a boys' group." He was starting to get ticked. First she'd tried to tell him how to run his classroom. Now she was riding this Jeff guy. She should just return to her kitchen, manage away back there and let him and Jeff get on with their own things.

"I'll give him a break all right; right after his shift is over. Right now he's on my dime and I've not gotten any work out of him since you appeared."

"Your dime?" What did she mean, Rob wondered.

Jeff shifted his feet and looked down. "I'm not standing on your dime, Ellie. Yours or anyone else's."

Ellie rolled her eyes. "That's an idiom, Jeff. I didn't mean it literally."

"You mean he works for you?"

"Yes."

"Does he like fix those computers?" He pointed to the side wall.

"Among other things. Yes, he fixes stuff but he's also responsible for many of the smells in this place. You should come for lunch sometime and taste the deli sandwiches Jeff creates."

Jeff launched into a detailed explanation of the meats he planned to cook for the rest of the week, in far, far more detail than Rob ever wanted to hear about any culinary effort.

Ellie approached, holding her arm out and palm up, facing Jeff. "That's TMI, Jeff. The short version would do."

"TMI?" asked Rob.

"That's what she says when she's too lazy to say 'too much information'," explained Jeff. "She probably shouldn't butcher the language that way but she uses it as a signal to tell me when customers don't want the full story. It's not always easy to know how much to tell them. If they ask things like, "Where did this delicious meat come from?" I tell them. Sometimes I'm only part-way through the explanation and they stop making eye contact. Did you know that some people have short attention spans? They ask a question then can't remain focused long enough to get a proper answer. It's not just eye contact you have to watch for. Sometimes they stop eating and stare at the table. Shoulders give you clues as well. Their shoulder may drop down or it'll turn away from you. You gotta watch for things like that, even when it doesn't make sense. I mean, if someone asks, isn't it only polite to give an answer?"

The temptation to shake his head was strong in Rob's mind; shake it to see if his brains would rattle. Following this conversation was hard. He glanced at Ellie to see if she was having the same trouble.

Blast that woman. She was grinning. At him. Was she actually trying not to laugh at him? Ellie turned her gaze to Jeff and the two of them exchanged broad smiles.

"I did it again, didn't I, Ellie?" Jeff asked her.

"Yep." Neither of them seemed to mind, though. The only one uncomfortable was Jeff. But then, when had he not been uncomfortable in this woman's presence? Ellie and Jeff must have known each other a long time to be this relaxed together. Or, maybe they had a thing going on. He looked more closely at the two of them. He wasn't getting any back-off vibes from Jeff, but then again, he likely didn't see him as any threat. It was pretty obvious that Rob and Ellie rubbed each other the wrong way.

Anyway, they needed to get rolling. He turned to Jeff. "What time do you get off work?"

Ellie replied for him. "In about twenty minutes."

"Ellie, your watch is off again," Jeff told her after checking the time on his own watch. "In exactly seventeen minutes and forty-six seconds we close down."

Was Ellie that much of a task master boss that Jeff needed to be absolutely precise, Rob wondered?

Jeff continued. "I told you that you should get an atomic watch like mine. It corrects itself to a fraction of a second so you never need to wonder about the time." He turned to Jeff. "Some people have problems with time, you know. They try to say 'about' or 'roughly'. There actually is no 'about' with time. Time either is or it isn't. It's measurable. If we all used atomic watches there would be no confusion over this 'about' stuff. What does that even mean, anyway? If you say 'about twenty minutes' do you mean eighteen minutes or twenty-two minutes? There's a difference, you know."

Ellie cut him off. "And we've just lost another four of those precious minutes talking about it. Let's get this place shut down, and then you're free to go." They stood back out of the way as the last customers went out the door.

"Anything I can do to help?" Rob asked, and then wondered where that had come from.

"Sure," said Ellie. "You can empty the coffee machines and rinse them out. I'll bus the tables and get the dishwasher going. Jeff needs to get his stuff ready for the morning and put the espresso machine back together."

Chapter 7

Once again, Rob found himself standing at the door to the bakery with Jeff, but this time Ellie was beside them. She looked different, younger, softer and better out of her starched whites and in a t-shirt and jeans.

Once on the street they loitered a minute, then Ellie said, "Well, I'd better let you guys get on your way. See you tomorrow, Jeff."

Jeff remembered his manners. "Why don't you come with us, Ellie? It's not good to feel left out. Three is an okay number. I don't know how much this guy knows so maybe you can help us. You know, interpret or explain stuff to him if I get too technical."

The laughter came out of Ellie's mouth. Rob thought it was probably at his expense but her laughter was infectious. He couldn't be mad, at least not this once.

"Sure," he echoed. "Why not come along? You've never been shy about giving me instructions before so I don't see why you should start now."

Ellie was unsure how to take this and was prepared for a fight. "Jeez, Louise. How many times do I have to apologize for that? I was wrong, all right? I jumped to some conclusions in my attempt to help Sara and her kid. Cut me some slack, why don't you?"

She stopped as she checked out Rob's face and caught his grin. Was he having her on? Did this guy actually have a sense of humor? She slowly returned his smile and suddenly it was all right.

"Sure. I've got nothing better to do right now. I was going to go home and nap, but you can sleep when you're dead, right?" Ellie took an arm of each guy and they started off toward Jeff's place.

"Well, you can't actually liken death to sleeping. Our culture has a lot of euphemisms for death, but sleep isn't one of them unless you add an adjective like permanent sleep," Jeff explained.

Ellie grinned at them both and sauntered down the street arm in arm as Jeff continued his discourse on society's illogical views on death.

"Do you walk to work every day?" Rob asked Jeff.

"Yes."

Jeff's home was *not* close by. When they had started walking from the bakery, Rob assumed that they'd be going a few blocks, half a dozen at most. But they were still walking forty-five minutes later.

Ellie sensed his unease and squeezed his arm. "It's not much farther now," she said.

"Twenty-three more houses to be exact," Jeff said.

"If it's this far, why didn't we take my car?" Rob wondered.

"You have a car? Did you drive to the bakery?" Jeff asked.

"Yes, I parked around the corner."

"Why didn't you say so?" questioned Jeff. "I can't read your mind, you know. You didn't say anything about a car, so how would I know? You have to tell people things or they can't guess. We'd have been in front of the computers by now if you had suggested we drive instead of walk."

"Yeah, Rob, yeah. What was the matter with you? We could have been there already." Ellie could hardly contain her grin. If she wasn't ripping into him, she was ribbing him.

Rob sighed. "Sorry, guys. I didn't know. I assumed you lived close by."

"Close is a relative term. If you think nationally or globally, then yes, I do live close to the bakery. If you're an arachnid making the trek, then I do not live close and it would be a long, long walk."

Rob just looked at him. Jeff thought that Rob was unfamiliar the word. "Arachnid is the proper term for what you might know as a spider," he explained.

Rob then looked from Jeff to Ellie. She was having the time of her life. Why was she so relaxed around this guy? Then it came to him. Mel had told him about her brother, her brother with Asperger's Syndrome. Asperger's was on the autism spectrum. This must be the same fellow. Ah, that explained some things - like his precise language, conspicuous use of social niceties and tendency to deliver speeches when he was on a topic he enjoyed.

Changing the subject, Rob asked, "How long have you two known each other?"

"We met some time after Ben and Mel started seeing each other, so it's been less than a year, right?" Ellie asked Jeff.

There was a slight pause, and then Jeff said, "ten months, one week and three days."

Embarrassment washed over Rob. What was the matter with him? Look how at ease Ellie was with Jeff. She was a baker, just a lay person, while he was the one with the post-graduate special education training. He'd taken classes in working with students with autism spectrum disorders. He'd taught these kids for years now. How could he get on their wavelengths and do so well with them, but not be comfortable with an adult with autism? What was different?

He thought about it as they cruised by the houses, Jeff counting them off as they walked. When he got a new group of students, Rob knew in advance which kids had autism or any other learning difference. He made sure to read the cumulative files and any reports in those files. Did that give him preconceived notions about those kids? About what they could do? What to expect from them? He did it so he'd be prepared, have ready the things that each child needed to feel comfortable and be successful. There was very little the kids did that could throw him.

But Jeff, this man of about his own age, was a different story. Rob had lost that at-ease feeling he usually had around kids with unique styles. Rob was not sure this said anything good about himself. Did he feel superior and in charge around kids? That he had a lot to offer them?

But Jeff it seemed had something to offer Rob - maybe a whole lot of somethings. He certainly seemed like a smart guy, talented on many fronts.

Rob thought about Ellie, relaxed walking between these two men, holding their arms, joking with Jeff. It's not as if they had known each other forever, ten months or so as Jeff had informed them, but Ellie accepted Jeff like an old friend. Their banter was companionable, their trust obvious. Jeff actually seemed to like Ellie and Rob was beginning to see why.

When she wasn't attacking him, she was, well, nice. Attractive even. She had an easy acceptance of people. And, to her credit, when she'd launched into him at the school, she had been trying to help a couple people who were almost strangers to her. Watching her out of the corner of his eye, there was that grin on her face that hinted at mischief now that he had gotten to know her better.

Know her better? What was up with that? This was the woman he'd sworn to avoid at all costs just last week. Was he actually thinking of ways to spend more time with her to get to know more about her?

Chapter 8

The three of them clomped down the stairs to the basement of Jeff's parents' home. Rob looked around in the dim light. "You live here?" he asked.

"Sure. Well mostly. I have a bedroom over there," he gestured behind them," but it's not used very much. Usually I bunk down there," pointed at a futon messed with a quilt and a pillow. Hard to say what color the quilt might have once been but the colors on the pillow were clearer - the middle had a large yellow stain, probably where Jeff's head had lain many, many times. The whole basement had that funky smell that went along with heavy use, closed windows and questionable cleaning practices.

"You live here alone?" he asked Jeff.

"Yeah, but my parents live upstairs. I mostly eat with them. My Mom insists. She's positive I can't feed myself properly even though I'm a way better cook than she is."

Rob could understand Mrs. Nicol's misgivings. On the other hand, he'd sampled some of Jeff's cooking at the bakery and it had been without a doubt stupendous. He really could cook.

"I think I'll go say hello to your parents," said Ellie.

"Why? Jeff asked her.

"To let them know we're here."

"They know. Do you think that we tip-toed in? They heard us, I'm sure. Mom says she always listens for comings and goings as she calls it."

"It's still polite for me to go say hello to Mr. and Mrs. Nicols."

"Oh." This surprised Jeff. "Well, say hello to them for me, too." Jeff looked expectantly at Rob.

"Ah, yeah, and for me, too," echoed Rob uncomfortably.

Ellie stifled her laughter and said, "Sure." Rob could tell that she was smirking as she retreated back up the stairs. She really did like having a laugh at his expense, didn't she?

Jeff started in on their plans. He didn't offer Rob a seat, something to drink or tell him where the bathroom was. He was all business.

"So," Jeff asked. "Do you want to jump right in along with your boys' group or do you want to practice ahead of time?"

"What do you suggest?"

"That depends on how smart you are. How technical you are. Have you done much programming? Built many computers?"

"Neither."

Jeff looked disappointed. "Well, what do you know? You at least do your own upgrades, don't you - replace the hard drive, add RAM, swap out drives...?"

"Yeah, I know how to do stuff like that, just basic things the average guy can do."

"Average? I don't have much concept of average. I've found that what I think is common, basic knowledge everyone should have is not that common at all. You shouldn't be allowed to have a computer if you don't know how to take care of it. If you don't understand how a thing runs, you don't deserve to have it."

"I'm not sure that's fair. The typical person can use a computer for years without having to know those things. Besides, they can pay people to fix it when things go wrong."

"What a cop out." Jeff shook his head. He continued. "I don't have time to figure out all that you know or more likely, don't know," Jeff told Rob.

Rob tried to get the conversation back on to what he needed, rather than on his personal deficiencies, which he's sure would be numerous in Jeff's estimation. "Mel told me that that I should look at Linux for an operating system if I wanted the kids to build computers on a shoestring."

"On a shoestring? Why would she say that? I can't think of any use for a shoelace in a computer. Tying components in would not be stable enough." Jeff shook his head. "Sometimes Mel doesn't make a lot of sense."

Before Rob could explain or even try to follow this train of thought, Jeff went on. "She's right about choosing Linux instead of a Mac OS or a Windows box, but you can't just say Linux. Linux is an operating system, sure and many versions are free or close to free, but there are all kinds of Linux distros, some for newbies, some for home, some for professional use, some for servers and some for programmers. Which do you want?"

"How should I know?"

Jeff rolled his chair over to another computer. He woke it up with the touch of a mouse, and called up a website. His fingers flew faster than Rob could read the letters that appeared on the screen.

"Here," Jeff told him. "Take this online test. It'll assess your knowledge level, what you plan to do on the computer then suggest which Linux distro might be best for your needs."

"You keep saying distro. What's distro mean again?" Rob asked. "Distro is short for distribution. Really, it means who you get it from, the copy of your Linux operating system, I mean. Now, take this test and we'll see which distro it recommends for you."

Rob turned his attention to the Linux Distribution Chooser test (http://www.zegeniestudios.net/ldc/index.php?lang=en).

"Okay, I'm finished. And based on the answers I chose, the program narrows it down to four different Linux operating systems." Now that he'd gotten this far, Rob had no idea how to proceed.

"Did you read through them? Choose one?"

"Yeah, I read through all the descriptions but that didn't help. Half of this is like reading Greek to me."

"So, what did you do next? Did you look any of them up? Compare the pros and cons?"

"Well, no. I was sort of hoping you'd help me with that."

Jeff sighed. "I can only hold your hand so far. You're going to have to do some of the work yourself. You're the person who's going to live with this distro so you should tailor it to you needs."

"I don't know where to begin."

Jeff's chair slid over again and his fingers flew over the keys. "Maybe we'd better start at the very beginning." To himself he muttered, you'd think Mel wouldn't have sent me someone this green. She knows I have no patience with people too lazy to learn. "Here," he said as if Rob would not have been able to hear what he just said. "Read through this," and he pulled up a website called, What is Linux and Why Is It So Popular?.

Chapter 9

The light evening breeze beckoned and Sara couldn't stand the thought of staying cooped up. It was the weekend and what did it matter if Ethan's bedtime was extended a bit. The fresh air might even help him sleep better. The park a few blocks away awaited them. She zipped Ethan into his new blue jacket and perched the grey, knit cap on his head.

The park bordered a residential area, then stretched into the hills and wooded areas surrounding the edge of the city. It was a calm place, an oasis for urban-dwellers. Sara wished she knew what sorts of birds were singing; one day when she had time, she'd find out.

She headed for a bench, not too far from the swings and climbing equipment. There were a couple kids playing and she assumed Ethan would go join them. The thump against her back told her otherwise. Ethan pushed up against her side.

"Go on, son. Go play with the kids. Doesn't it look like fun?"

Ethan shook his head back and forth.

"Sure, it'll be fun. Look. See that little girl on the swing? She looks like she's having fun." Ethan didn't budge. Sigh. This was not going to go well. She took his hand. "Come on. I'll go with you." It took a little tug, but Ethan trailed behind her, over to the swing set.

With some encouragement and coaxing, Ethan clambered onto the swing and submitted to his mother's pushes. But, her bench and her book beckoned, so Sara instructed Ethan to swing himself now.

From time to time, Sara would glance up. Ethan propelled himself in a desultory fashion, never seeming to achieve that graceful coordination of leaning into the swing's forward arc and pushing back with his legs.

The next time Sara glanced up, she tensed when she didn't see her son on the swings. Oh, there he was. He'd followed the little girl to the slide. Good. She went back to her story.

The giggles caught her attention as the other child spread her arms wide and zoomed down the slide. Sara smiled. Ethan stood at the bottom of the ladder, ready for his turn, but hesitating. The girl ran around and stood behind Ethan. She waited, and then poked him in the back. "Get going," she said.

Sara could see Ethan stiffen. She rose to intervene, knowing what could come next. But, she sat back down when Ethan stepped out of the way to let the girl have another turn. He stood watching her. He'd take his turn next, she was sure.

The next noises Sara heard voices deeper than those of the couple children around Ethan. Three boys several years older than Ethan milled around the swings now. Sara stood to see over them to spy Ethan. His bright, blue jacket should stand out. No, she couldn't see him. Since there was an assortment of climbing equipment in the playground, she wasn't worried; he could be playing on any on it. She sauntered around the area, looking in all the small spaces. No Ethan.

She turned toward the older boys. They were loud and laughing and posturing the way of wannabe punks. What were they saying? They were laughing about the little dweeb. One slapped his buddy on the back as they chortled and pointed in the distance. Sara followed his point and off in the distance, on the hill's upward slope was a blue jacket, moving steadily away.

Ethan! She screamed his name. All activity in the play area stilled. Sara pointed toward the rapidly retreating figure. "Get him," she yelled. "He's running away. Help!" She took off after him.

The older boys looked at one another, then took off after Sara. They had youth and excess energy on their sides and quickly overtook her. Much of Sara's breath was taken up with calling Ethan's name.

Was he slowing? Maybe. As he climbed the rise of the hill, he glanced over his shoulder. He stopped as he saw the three boys pounding after him, then took off again, faster than ever.

But a frightened six year old is no match for almost-teenaged boys who were enjoying the thrill of the chase. As Ethan passed the crest of the hill, just out of Sara's sight, the boys caught up with him. Now that they'd achieved their goal, they didn't quite know what to do with him. No one had given them instructions. Uncertain, they surrounded Ethan. As he tried to escape their circle, one grabbed him by the arm. "Hey. That lady told you to stop or come back."

Ethan struggled in his grip and when he would have slid away, a second boy grabbed the back of his jacket and held on. "Settle down, kid. We're not going to hurt you. We'll just take you back to that lady. Is she your mom?"

There was no response. The kid shook the back of Ethan's jacket. "Kid. I'm talking to you. Is that lady your mom?" He looked at his friends. They'd all had the lectures about stranger danger when they were younger. Was something like that going on here? Were they supposed to give the kid back to the lady or protect him from her? The same thoughts went through all of their minds.

Puffing and calling, Sara made her way up the last part of the hill. "Oh, thank god," she huffed between sucking breaths. "Thank you!" She fell to her knees in front of Ethan and held out her arms. Ethan threw himself into her embrace and held on and held on. After several seconds, she raised her eyes to take in the young men around them. "Thank you for catching him. He was so scared. When he gets overwhelmed, he just takes off but he doesn't know where he's going and could get lost or hurt. You saved him." She released Ethan and rose to her feet but kept firm hands on her son's shoulders. To the boys she said, "You are heroes and might have saved Ethan from harm. You should be proud of yourselves."

The youth puffed up, their cockiness ratcheted up several notches as they sauntered back down the hill, making up the stories they'd tell to their buddies.

Chapter 10

Rob and Jeff still labored on in the basement, sometimes Jeff patiently explaining, sometimes not. Every so often Ellie would chime in, "He wants the short version, Jeff. He's never going to be a programmer. He just wants to use the system and show kids how to use it."

"I know, I know," Jeff would reply, "but the beauty of this is that there is so much more to it. Sure, you can just use Linux the way you would a Windows box. But don't you want to take a look under the hood?"

He'd get a resounding, "No!" from both Ellie and Rob. To Rob's surprise, Ellie knew a fair bit about this. Initially, she'd been intrigued by the concept of a free operating system, given the cost of buying the popular systems on the market. She was astounded to learn that hundreds of extra dollars were tacked onto the cost of a new computer just for the operating system when there was an equivalent free or for under twenty-five dollars.

Too chicken to try it out on her main computer, she had an older one in her closet that had been owned by one of her brothers before he left home. She crossed her fingers and wiped that hard drive clean. Then, having downloaded a Linux distro called OpenSuSE (http://www.opensuse.org/en/) onto a DVD and inserted it into the computer. After clicks and whirls and waiting, it worked! She had an up and running computer without paying hundreds of dollars on an operating system. After playing with it for a few months, Ellie became so comfortable with its speed and ease of operation, not to mention its stability, that she removed the operating system that had come with her laptop and installed Linux as its operating system. She avoided the programming geek versions of Linux and kept to those which were kind to inexperienced users. What she looked for in an operating system was one that allowed her to carry on as if it was not even there. To her mind, the job of operating systems was to work away in the background without any input from her, letting her just plain use the computer as she pleased.

For a guy who used to think he wasn't bad with computers, Rob felt left out. Humbled as he was, he still saw a problem. "So, I collect old computers and even if I get Linux thrown on them, or help the kids do it themselves, then what? It's not enough to say we have computers with operating systems. We have to be able to use them. Part of the point is in helping the kids learn the skills of building a computer, then letting take them home. For most of these kids there is no computer at home when they need to do homework. We don't have the budget to buy software any more than we do to buy operating systems."

"So, use Apache's Open Office®."

"What's Open Office®?"

"It's what I use to make the menus at the bakery and to keep inventory and send invoices," said Ellie. It's a complete suite of tools, pretty close to Microsoft Office®, but it's free. It has a word processor, spread sheet, database and presentation software. And, if I create something in Open Office® then go somewhere where there's only Microsoft Office® available, my Open Office® stuff opens in the other program and reads it just fine. And oh, did I mention that it's free?"

"Free as in legally free? I can't be doing anything against the law with these kids," worried Rob.

"Take a look," Jeff said as his fingers on the keyboard too them to http://www.openoffice.org/.

Ellie surfed the web while Rob read and Jeff tapped away on his own computer. There were no shortage of computers in this basement; they could have had three other people here, each with a machine of their own to use. When he shut down the website, Rob looked through files until he found that Open Office® was indeed installed on this computer. He started it and played around a while.

"Okay, I'm convinced about this part of it. Open Office® would definitely work for these kids' needs throughout high school and college, too. But they need to use a computer for more than just word processing and the stuff that Open Office® does. Email is a part of our lives. How are they going to search the internet? I looked and I don't see anything that looks like Internet Explorer®."

"They'll do it the same way you were just using the internet," said Jeff. "Internet Explorer® is only one example of a browser. I think the machine you're on uses Safari®." He slid over and looked. "Yep. Again, it's free and will work fine with Linux."

"Then what about email? I don't see any form of Outlook® here."

Jeff gave him a few examples of free, web-based emails he could use.

Rob was not quite sold on this "free" stuff yet. "But what about viruses, spyware and other malicious software we have to protect ourselves from online?"

"That's the beauty of Linux. It's really rare for anyone's Linux machine to be attacked or get hacked."

"Why's that?"

"Think about it."

Rob had been trying, truly trying to think for the past two hours but was coming to his limit, Ellie could tell. She took over from Jeff. "Those nasty beasties who create viruses and worms and those things program to attack the largest number of computers they can reach. What's the most common operating system?"

That Rob knew. "Windows, like Windows Vista® or 10."

"Right. And who gets almost all the viruses and stuff - Windows users. At one time MAC users felt fairly immune but now they have some trouble as well. But Linux users, well it's extremely rare for them to be bothered."

"But just to be sure," Jeff added, "there are lots of free anti-virus programs you can install." He was about to launch into a list of them when Rob put up his hand.

"Enough. My mind's boggling. I believe you, but I think I've learned enough for tonight. I'd better head out now, but can I give you a call when I have more questions?"

"No," was Jeff's answer.

"NO? Oh, sorry, I realize I've taken up a lot of your time and I appreciate all your help. You've steered me in the right direction and I'll try to take it from here." He stopped, because Jeff was scribbling on a paper, paying no attention to Rob whatsoever.

Jeff swiveled his chair back to face Rob, handing him the paper. "Here. I don't have a phone. Email me or if you really need the face-to-face thing, use Skype®. Other than that, I'm at the bakery every day. Bye." Then he turned back to his computer and became lost in his typing.

Ellie said, "I guess that's our cue." As they walked toward the stairs, she said, "See you tomorrow, Jeff."

A slight lifting of his hand from the keyboard indicated that Jeff had heard them and responded.

Chapter 11

"So, did you learn what you needed to?" Ellie asked Rob.

"That and then some. If you had the time to just sit and soak up his knowledge, it would be amazing. I thought I wasn't bad with computers but now I see that I know nothing compared to him. Sometimes I thought he was good at bringing things down to my level but at others he'd go on and on, way over my head. I had had this faint hope that he might be willing to help the kids with this project but now I doubt it. He'd lose them within the first few minutes."

"Don't be too sure about that. With you, he was trying to find your comfort level. Once he knows that, he can tailor what he says to fit your needs. With the kids, if he knew they were rudimentary gamers but had no experience with the insides of what makes a computer tick, he could teach them a lot. He's pretty systematic and could lead them along. I wouldn't rule it out."

They were standing in the driveway of the Nicols` home, under the reflection of a street light. Rob looked down the street in the direction they'd taken to get here. "I really wish I'd brought my car."

"Do we want to get into that again?" Ellie teased as she started walking.

"No. I've had enough of having my short-comings throw into my face for one night." When they got to the end of the driveway, he asked, "Where do you live?"

"A few blocks the other side of the bakery. It's not a bad jaunt to work in the mornings, just enough to wake me up."

"I'd offer to drive you home if I had my car here. Once we get back to my car, I can give you a ride from there. Or would you prefer that we call a taxi?"

"It's a nice night. Let's walk," and she took his arm again, just like she had with he and Jeff on the walk here. They continued in companionable silence, something Rob could never have imagined even earlier this day. Feeling relaxed around Ellie? Choosing to walk somewhere with her? Letting her touch him and actually liking it?

Ellie was not one to let things lie. "So, is this a good time to try to apologize again?"

Rob sighed. "It's a peaceful evening. Can't we just let things be?"

"No! You never did let me tell you how sorry I was for misjudging you. I hate injustice and I tend to jump in, sometimes without waiting to gather all the facts. I didn't know you at that time. If I had known you, I'd have realized that you would not be out to get Sara or her son."

Rob pulled back his head, raised one eyebrow and looked down at her. "Out to get them?"

"You know what I mean. The stuff that happened at their other school. What was going on there, by the way? I don't get it."

"Hard to speak for someone else, but the 'don't get it' you mentioned might have been happening there. When you're working with kids on the autism spectrum it really helps if you can 'get it'. By that, I mean put yourself in their shoes. If you can imagine what it might feel like to be them, then you can put things in place to help them become more comfortable."

"What do you mean?"

"Take time for instance. Time is a very hard concept for most kids with autism. It's not exactly easy to grasp for any little kid, but it seems especially elusive for those on the spectrum as well as kids with other sorts of difficulties like attentional issues, learning disabilities, fetal alcohol syndrome, to name a few.

"See, most children, over time, develop an internal feeling for the passage of time. They sense how long five minutes is or a half hour or a week. When you say we'll have snack in five minutes, they know that that if pretty soon. It's not enough time to become thoroughly engrossed in something complex that you love to do, nor is it long to wait if your stomach is rumbling. But a child with autism who does not have that time sense will not realize that that's enough time to finish writing that sentence or to do two more math questions. He might panic, thinking he's going to be told to put his things away when he's not finished. The teacher told him to do those ten questions, so that's the rule and now he's not going to be able to complete the work, landing him in trouble, or worse, having it for homework. So a tantrum may ensue due to his frustration over the impending time limit."

"So what can you do about it?"

"Lots, but it's a slow process. You need to work on a couple things together like building a relationship with the kid so he trusts you and knows you're there to help. To start building a sense of time, you work on it constantly, pointing out how much time passed since you did the last thing, how much time we have until the next item on our schedule and using visuals."

"Visuals?"

"Kids with autism for the most part, take in what they see more easily than what they hear. So, instead of just talking about the passage of time, show it. I use something called a Time Timer® a lot. We have small, four inch ones for a kid's desk, some in watch form for individuals, a twelve inch one on the wall and I use one on the interactive white board all the time."

"How does that help?"

"Say we're starting a new subject in ten minutes. The timer shows ten minutes in bright red and the numbers slowly count down, the red section getting smaller until the time is up.

"We also run our lives in my class, by a schedule. Some kids use the words on the schedule, others go by the pictures. Do you use some kind of daily organizer in your business?"

"Definitely. I used to keep this book but now I do it all on my phone. I'd be sunk if I lost it. I have listed there all the things I need to do in the day and which I need to do first. Otherwise, I might forget an important step in the morning that will have ramifications for that afternoon. Like what if I forgot to get the dough rising first thing in the morning and didn't have any fresh buns for lunch so Jeff can create his sandwiches."

"Kids with autism have trouble making sense of their world. They often feel that things just come at them unexpectedly. They feel that they can't prepare themselves and don't know what might be expected of them. A visual schedule gives them a sense of order so they know what's coming next. They're not so on edge that way.

"I get it. Mel has these visual schedules all over their house for Kyle to follow. She says it cuts down on the amount of nagging parents have to do if they can just point the kid to the steps he needs to follow in the poster on the wall. At first I wondered where she was finding the time to make all these charts but then I looked closely at them. Honestly, some of them just aren't pretty and look like she scrawled them on the spur of the moment. When I asked her, she laughed and said that's exactly what she did. Kyle doesn't care. As long as he understands what she means, he can follow it. And you know, Mel is not very good at drawing - not at all. She's actually pretty bad at it, but she says as long as she tells Kyle what it means, he gets it and follows it. I have noticed a couple places where Kyle has drawn over top of her picture though, to make it look better. Mel doesn't care and said that Kyle is making it his own, which is a good thing."

"So, you get this and Mel gets this. My brother gets it and even I do to a certain extent. What was wrong with Ethan's last school? Why did he have so many problems there?"

"Just like parents, most teachers are doing the best they can at the time with the tools at their disposal. Some may lack experience with kids who learn differently or think differently. There may have been no one in their school to help, no one with some background in autism spectrum disorders.

"Pretty much every school nowadays has at least one special education teacher. But when most people took their university training, special education dealt with things like cerebral palsy, attentional difficulties, learning disabilities, intellectual disabilities. Little was known about teaching kids with autism even fifteen years ago. Since the prevalence rate for autism has burgeoned in the last decade or so, every teacher will encounter a student with autism and many are still unprepared for how to help. When the prevalence rate is one in every forty-two boys, every teacher can expect to have a student with autism.

"Look, most people who go into the teaching profession have strong verbal skills. We're talkers. At the older grades we tend to lecture, rightly or wrongly. Even in the younger grades where things are more visual and hands-on, we still tend to talk a lot. And when we get frustrated, most adults talk even more. We repeat ourselves, we raise our voices, and we use more words and all this goes over the head of the kid with autism."

They turned the last corner, walking onto the semi-commercial street where the bakery resided.

Rob continued. "Most kids on the autism spectrum have trouble with auditory processing, making sense out of what they hear and knowing how to act on it. Their ability to process what they hear goes down at times of stress or when there's a lot of background noise. Think about the most difficult times in schools for these kids - in the gymnasium, the hallways, the boot rooms, all noisy, confusing places."

"Mel insists that they have a routine for everything they do at home."

"Exactly. That way Kyle knows what's expected of him. He doesn't freeze in uncertainty or have a meltdown out of frustration when he can't figure things out. It takes time to teach the routine but it is well worth the time and effort for everyone concerned."

"But then Mel does things to purposely mess up the routine. At first Ben objected; he thought it was being mean to Kyle."

Rob laughed. "Yeah, I can see how someone could think that. But first you teach the rules and the routine. We always, always do it this way. Then you need to teach change because no matter how hard you try, life still throws curve balls and your nice little routine gets disrupted. If you don't teach a child how to adapt and live through that change, then they're hooped when it happens, especially if you're not around to guide them through it."

"Kyle has certainly had lots of disruptions to the routine Ben created - like a fire in their kitchen, cutting a gash in his head and going to the emergency room for stitches, getting lost, moving like three times in one year. And meeting a new father."

"But the best thing out of all that was that Kyle got to meet his new auntie - me!"

"I take it you see that as a good thing for him?"

Ellie's elbow dug into his stomach. "Jerk," she told him but her smile told him she knew he was teasing. This was a different Ellie than Rob had seen before - a far different Ellie than the siren who'd launched into him in Mel's room that first day. This Ellie was more like the woman who bantered with Jeff and probably the Aunt Ellie that Kyle loved. She really wasn't as bad as he'd originally thought and tonight had been fun. He'd almost be sorry when it was over.

The neon sign for the bakery was visible just a block or so up ahead. Soon their walk would be over. Rob was surprised that that realization disappointed him. He was actually having a good time with Ellie, unbelievable as that seemed.

"Where exactly do you live from here?" he asked her.

Ellie withdrew her hand from his arm and pointed. "You take the first right after the bakery, then carry on for one and a half blocks."

When she lowered her arm, Rob grasped her hand and pulled it again through his arm. He kept his other hand over hers. She looked at him, but didn't pull away.

"Do you have house, apartment or what?" he asked her.

"I live in the suite over my parents' garage. Years ago that was part of the head baker's perks, getting free rent in exchange for less pay and horrendous hours. When he retired to go live with his daughter in Florida, my father tried taking over his duties and it was a disaster. Dad used to specialize in some of the bakery items, especially the donuts but little else. When he found that he was not that good at the other baking, he increased our output of donuts. He made great donuts, for sure, but as people became more health conscious they ate fewer donuts and wanted more choices when they came into the bakery."

"So what did you do?"

"It took a lot of work but I convinced dad to let me try my hand at the baking. He didn't seem to realize that for years I'd been working under Clive, our former baker, and in his later years, I'd done it all. He really wasn't here more than in name only, but dad didn't know that. I worked hard and I…"

"And modest, too."

"I'm not bragging, just stating the facts. I love it and have studied hard to get better and better. Unlike dad, I'm responsive to the market and make what people like. Dad fought me every step when I tried to change this place into a bistro. He wanted coffee, plain old coffee, none of this latte, espresso kind of stuff. But, that's what draws people in."

"It looked like business was thriving when I was there today."

"It is. It actually is, especially over lunch hour. Bringing in Jeff was the best move I ever made. He spent hours watching cooking shows on television, drinking in all that information. You may have noticed, but nothing is ever lost on Jeff - once he learns it, it's in there forever. Luckily for me, his knowledge of meats is extensive and he cooks up something different every day for sandwiches. We keep it simple, but fresh and delicious."

"So, Jeff is a computer genius plus a cook? What did he do before coming to work for you?"

"Not much of anything, from what I gather."

"Nothing? How could that be? He looks like he's what, in his early thirties?"

Ellie nodded. I think he'd tried a few short-term jobs but didn't find anything that suited him. He attended college for a while but didn't stick with that either, until Mel found him mostly online programs, which he aced. I gather that his parents are pretty protective of him and were just as content if he remained in their basement, under their eye. Mel says they were afraid that the world would be hard on him or that he'd have trouble coping."

"How'd he end up at your place?"

"Mel's doing again. The day she helped Ben, Kyle and their housekeeper, Millie move into the penthouse, she arranged for Jeff to cook for them. Ben was so impressed with the food that he called me. Once I'd sampled what Jeff could do, I begged him to come help at the bakery. We needed something to pull in the lunchtime crowd."

"Was this something he wanted to do?"

"I'm not sure he was looking for a job, but what he really wanted to do was cook. His mother rarely let him use her kitchen. Occasionally he'd go to Mel's place to use hers but he wanted free reign over a kitchen every day. I provided that."

"How was it going from not working to working every day for you?"

"We had lots of discussions that first week and some things to work out. Once Jeff learned what my rules were, he added a few of his own and we've gotten along great ever since. He's reliable and creative. At first I worried about the expense of the cuts of meat he chose but once his roasts were simmering in the oven and customers smelled the aromas, we sold out of sandwiches every day.

"I worried at first that Jeff really didn't care that much what the customers said they liked. He cooked what he wanted to cook. But there's variety and choice that everyone's happy and business has never been better."

"Your dad must have gotten over any of his old ideas then."

"Not really, but Mom's convinced him to come in less and less. Kyle has helped with that. He loves having a grandson nearby. Dad no longer asks to look at the books. Instead, I think he sees nearly all the tables full and that tells him enough.

"Another thing," Ellie continued. "When I first started selling different types of coffee, all I could afford was second-hand equipment. It broke down all the time. Well, some of it still does, but not for long. Jeff is a whiz at fixing anything and our equipment's never been in better shape."

"How do Mel and Jeff's parents feel about all this if they were overprotective and wanting to keep him at home?"

"I'm not sure that it matters. At first they were definitely not in favor and came to talk to me about it. Mrs. Nicols explained to me that Jeff is not like other young men because he has autism. She wanted to make sure I would not take advantage of her son or treat him badly. As if!"

Rob smiled at her indignation. Now that he was getting to know Ellie, he could not imagine her treating anyone badly. Well, maybe anyone besides himself, he thought, remembering their first meeting.

"Mel, I gather, had been fighting with her parents for years, trying to get them to loosen their reins on Jeff. I guess Jeff had had a couple lousy experiences many years ago with a bad boss. But, who hasn't had that happen to them? You learn and move on. At the bakery Jeff is getting to do what he wants to do. He's not keen on having to come in so early but once he realized that the meat had to be cooked and ready for the lunch crowd, he's never missed a day and never late."

"It sounds win-win for both of you."

"Definitely for me and good I think for Jeff, too. Probably if it wasn't good for him, Jeff would just not show up anymore. I think his parents have relaxed about it, too. At first they came by almost every day, staying for hours, watching Jeff and how he was treated. I treat him exactly the same as I do the rest of my staff. Besides, he's family now. We kid around and give each other a hard time. The Nicols must have gotten that message because they're usually only here on Saturdays now, when Mel and Ben bring Kyle in."

They were in front of Ellie's house now. They'd walked right by Rob's car and he hadn't even noticed.

"How could I have done that? I meant to stop at my car and drive you the rest of the way home. We didn't have to walk all this way. I don't know how I didn't notice."

Ellie laughed. "Maybe you were having too much fun with the enemy?"

"Yeah, I guess that was it. I did have fun. After our shaky beginning, I never thought I'd say that to you."

"Me, too, after thinking you were being nasty and ruining Sara and Ethan's lives," she said, grinning back at him. "Want to come up for a few minutes?"

"Tempting. But, I think I should be getting home. I have a lot of work to do prepping for the boys' group tomorrow."

There was an awkward pause, the first uncomfortable moment they'd had.

Ellie, ever forthright, said, "Maybe we should do this again some time."

"You mean you, me and Jeff?"

"Well that's not exactly what I had in mind, but something like that, sure."

"Can I call you sometime?"

"Sure. I'm in the book, but it's easiest to get me at the bakery. I'm there every day but I go to bed early. This is considered a late night for me."

"That must make dating tough."

"Who has time for dating?"

"Maybe I could convince you to make an exception."

"You know, you just might be one of the few guys who could. See ya.

"Night, and thanks for the good time."

Chapter 12

"Mrs. Fellows, may I speak with you a moment, please?"

Sara looked at her son's teacher and hesitated. "We're in a bit of a hurry - errands to run and that sort of thing."

"This won't take too long and it's important." Rob could almost see Ethan's mother squirm, much like her son did when put on the spot. To make it easier for her, he added, "I need your help and advice."

Mel appeared at the door, standing aside as the last of Rob's students left the room. "Hi, Mrs. Fellows," she introduced herself. "I'm Mel Wickens, the kindergarten teacher and also a parent of one of Ethan's friends in this class. Rob asked if Ethan and I would spend some time together in my room next door while you two talked. Would that be all right with you? Ethan already knows me, don't you, big guy?" She ruffled Ethan's hair and he leaned in to her. Mel gave him a firm squeeze against her side.

Still reluctant, Sara relented. "Just for a couple minutes, then we have to be getting on our way. Is that all right with you, son?" Without responding, Ethan reached for Mel's hand and started down the hall.

Rob grinned. "None of my kids ever mind going to Mel's room. She has the coolest toys in there and six year olds aren't that very different than five year olds."

When they were seated, he began. "I really do need your help with something. You're the expert on Ethan; I'm only just getting to know him. I may know a lot about teaching and six year olds and about autism, but each kid is unique and you're my best key to what makes Ethan tick.

"Today, he ran away," he continued then waited for Sara's reaction.

Her indrawn breath came quickly then her eyes flickered to the doorway where her son had stood moments ago.

"He's all right, you saw that yourself," Rob reassured her. "But I thought you should know. We caught him quickly and he was fine but we want to make sure he's always fine. Tell me, is this the first time he's run or has this happened before?"

Sara hesitated. Rob could see a multitude of answers pouring through her mind. "We're all on the same side here," he reminded her. "We want what is best for Ethan, not just in this school year but in the future."

With her eyes on the desk between them, Sara admitted, "This is not the first time, no. At his last school it happened a lot. That's some of the reason they would ask me to come get him, when they were short-staffed and didn't have someone available who could run after him.

Then it started coming out in a rush. "But it wasn't just the school's fault. It happens with me, too. I'm in a panic half the time when we go shopping. What if I lose him? What if I can't catch him? What if my back is turned just for a half second and he bolts and I don't see which direction he took? What if some stranger sees this little boy alone and takes him? I don't know what to do."

"Okay, we'll work on this together. We have the same goals - neither of us wants Ethan to bolt and we all want to keep him safe." He pushed the box of tissues closer to Sara. Her tears had started and her head remained down. "Can you tell me about when he runs?" he asked.

Sara started on a different track. "It's my fault. My husband tells me that all the time. I started it, he says and now I have to live with it."

Rob just waited. When she seemed to need encouragement, he asked, "How do you think it started?"

"When Ethan was little I started this game. You have to understand how hard it was when he was small. Everyone dreams of this baby you'll sit with and cuddle. But Ethan wasn't like that. He didn't seem to like me when he was a baby. He didn't want to be held. When he cried, I couldn't make him stop. Every baby wants his mother to comfort him, doesn't he? But not Ethan, at least not with me.

"No," she corrected. "It wasn't just me he didn't like. When my mother-in-law came over, she couldn't comfort him either. The whole grandma-in-the-rocking-chair-thing didn't work with Ethan." She swiped at her wet cheeks with another tissue.

"Other mothers talk about what a bonding experience nursing was, gazing into their child's face during feedings. Well, it didn't work that way with us. Sure, I'd gaze into his little face but he didn't look at me. His eyes wandered around, or if they did look at me, it wasn't at my eyes. He'd seem to stare a few seconds at my nose, then at an eyebrow, or parts of my face but not into my eyes the way other babies would. And he tolerated my holding him just until he was finished eating, then he'd squirm and fuss until I put him down. He'd actually prefer lying in a crib alone to being in his mother's arms."

Rob opened his mouth to say that he'd heard this many times before from parents of kids with autism, but Sara rushed on.

"Before he was born, I signed up for this mothers and tots play group. You sit around in a circle, sing songs, chant nursery rhymes, play in the swimming pool, all things normal babies love to do with their mothers. But I cancelled. How could I go when I'd be the only mother there who didn't know how to make her baby stop crying? The only mother whose baby hated to be held? The only mother whose baby hated her? Babies are supposed to give you unconditional love. Even lousy mothers have kids who love them and want them, but not mine."

This was more than Rob had bargained for. He was good at analyzing situations, finding out the reasons that might be behind the behaviors and at making a plan. The touchy-feely, sensitive stuff was not his forte. But, this woman was hurting and they would not be able to get onto the planning stage before spending time on some of this. Right at that moment, he wished he was in the kindergarten room playing with Ethan and Mel was in here with Mrs. Fellows. Suck it up, he told himself. You can do it. At least you can try not to make her feel worse.

"Mrs. Fellows, I've seen you with your son and I've seen how Ethan reacts to you. He loves you - it's obvious. His face lights up when you come for him at the end of the day. He wants to share with you what he's done." He saw her about to disparage that last comment and put up his hand. "I know, I know, he may not show it in the same way as some of the other kids, but he does want to share with you. How his day went may not come out in a rush of words, but he'll fish around in his back pack until he finds some paper he's worked on and hold that out to you. He's communicating. Not all communication is about words; in fact we convey far more with our body language and our actions than with our words. Ethan wants to show you what he's done. And, he always looks for a hug. He may have not when he was young, but he's grown into it now. Did you notice how he even leaned into Mel for a hug just before they left the room?"

Sara nodded. "A couple years ago he'd never have done that."

"His nervous system has matured," Rob explained. Sara's forehead creased, so he explained. "Many kids with autism seem to be wired differently. Their sensory systems can be over active or under active. With some kids, it takes a lot more stimulation to arouse them to a level where they respond. Others seem hyper-sensitive and over-react to things like touch, sounds, smells, noises and other things in their environment. They can't seem to filter out all the input coming at them. A baby's too young to explain to you or to run away from it all so they do the only thing they can - cry. For some, the normal jiggling and hugging we do to try to calm a baby may not help and may even increase their sense of being overwhelmed.

"Sometimes too, we're gentle with a baby, very gentle in our touch. That light, feathery touch can be calming to some kids, but is like fingernails on a blackboard to others. Before they left this classroom, did you notice how Mel hugged your son? There was nothing soft and gentle about it - Mel hugged him firmly. Did you see Ethan's reaction?"

Sara nodded. "He sort of melted into her. I hadn't thought about the different kinds of hugs before. Maybe that's why Ethan hates my mother. She's a very gentle sort and tries to brush his skin lightly. Even as a baby, he'd arch away from her and scream. But he was better with my dad, who's more of a gruff guy and held him solidly across his chest.

"He could not stand my father-in-law either. When Ethan was a baby, my husband's father really didn't have anything to do with him. Women looked after babies, in his mind. But when Ethan began walking around, he took more of an interest. He'd build these towers of wooden blocks and Ethan would knock them down. That's how they played together. But it would all end in screams when Jack would suddenly pick Ethan up and toss him in the air. Most little kids love that, but Ethan would scream and scream. It's not that he was ever dropped, not even close, but he hated that game. It got so bad that whenever his grandparents would come over, Ethan would start screaming or hide. They complained a lot to my husband about how I was raising Ethan so badly and making a sissy out of him.

Trying to get back on track, Rob asked, "You said that this started as a game. His running, I mean. What did you mean by that?"

"When he was little, it was so hard to relate to him or to get him to relate to me. What kind of a mother does not bond with her child? Well, that mother was me. I looked after him as best I could but we didn't really have that kind of mother-child bond you see in movies or read about in books, or watch other mothers having.

"So, whenever Ethan did respond to me I was elated. We started this game when I'd pretend to chase him. He'd run and giggle. He'd even look over his shoulder to see if I was coming, almost as if he wanted me to. It was one of the first things we ever did together, actually played together."

"Sounds like a pretty normal experience. Why do you sound like that's a problem?"

"Because it became a problem. My husband says that's where this whole running away thing came from, from me teaching him to run and having someone chase after him."

Rob contemplated a moment, trying to get the words right. "Mrs. Fellows, I don't have kids of my own but I'm around small children all day. On the playground, I'd say that half their games involve running or chasing. Kids do it all the time. When I visit my niece and nephews, I play chase games with them when I run after them, grab them and tickle them. They love it! So do I, for that matter. I bet most parents have played like that with their kids.

"The problem," he continued, "is that with kids with autism, they may not generalize in the same way. While my niece gets that this is just something we do in the house with Uncle Rob, I doubt she'd act the same way in a different setting with a different adult."

"That's exactly what Ethan has done. At his last school he ran the most from an Educational Associate he really liked."

"Why do you think he ran when he was at that school?"

"Sometimes he'd run, trying to play with her. But at other times he ran almost in a panic. They told me he'd run like demons were after him and have this terrified look. When they caught up to him, he'd be panting and sweating and his heart was racing, but it wasn't from the exertion because he never really did run that far. It was like he was scared and trying to get away from something."

"Most kids instinctively pick up the social rules, like when and where it's okay to do certain things, such as playing chase games. Children with autism spectrum disorders don't seem to automatically get these things and need to be taught the rules. And, when they do generalize on their own, they might get it wrong and not know how to self-correct that wrong perception, or even realize that it's wrong and that other kids don't act that way.

"Mrs. Fellows..."

"Sara," she interrupted. "Please call me Sara. You already know enough about me for us to be on a first name basis. One side of her mouth turned up as she said this. So, she did have a sense of humor and might be able to laugh at herself. Good to know. He might not need to tread so lightly.

"Okay, Sara. First, quit beating yourself up over playing a game with your son when he was younger. You've probably seen other parents play with their kid like that and maybe you even did it with your mother and father when you were his age. It's a normal thing to do. At that time you did not know that Ethan had autism. There was no way you could have guessed that he might take and run with this one aspect of your lives."

When Sara smiled at him, Rob thought back over what he'd just said and caught the unintended pun. "Sorry. You know what I mean, he added, then continued. "So, what started out as a fun thing to do with mom became over-generalized, for whatever reason and has now become a pattern."

Sara nodded.

"A pattern we don't want. Look, here are the things that concern me. One, while this may be a fun game for a two year old, it's no longer an appropriate kind of play for a six year old, at least not in the way Ethan's doing it. Two, it's not safe. Even when he's trying to have fun with someone, looking over his shoulder while he runs into the street could have disastrous consequences."

Sara's tears started again. "I know, I know. That's constantly on my mind. And, if anything happened, it would be all my fault." Her spine straightened. "But that's why his previous school had a one-to-one aide with him at all times, to keep him from running."

Rob's left eyebrow rose just a bit. "Did it work? Did it stop him from running?"

"Well, no, but when he did run there was someone watching who could run after him." But when they were short staffed, they would call her.

"Is that what you want? Do you also want a fence? Do you want him tethered to the ground or to an adult? Maybe he just shouldn't be allowed outside at all."

"Look here, Mr. Sells. My son deserves fresh air and exercise just like any other child, even if he does have autism and even if he does complicate your life."

"Yep, you're right. I absolutely agree. But how do we do that and at the same time keep him safe?"

"Get another aide to be with him at all times!"

"Hmm. That might work right now, although you did say that he still ran at his other school. Let's think about this a moment.

"Remember how kids with autism get into patterns?" He waited for Sara's nod. "What patterns are we helping him develop if we glue an adult to his side, one who will chase after him every time he runs?"

Sara sighed. "We might be reinforcing the same game I set up with him when he was younger."

"Yes. I'm sorry, but yes, that is most likely what we'd be doing. But, there's more. Apart from teaching him that this is one way to interact with that adult and that it's supposedly fun, how long could we continue this?"

"As long as is necessary to keep him safe."

"You and I have a pretty good idea how fast a six year old boy can run and we could both probably catch him. But Ethan is not going to stay six for long. Soon, he'll be ten then sixteen. Have you seen how fast teenaged boys can run?"

"But that's in the future. I'm worried about him now."

"Me, too. Remember about autism and patterns, though. When you and he started that chase game a few years ago, you were thinking about the fun you were having with your boy, not about the possible ramifications down the road." He watched Sara's face crumble. "I'm sorry. I don't mean to be hurtful, but it's the truth. You were doing what probably three-quarters of all parents do with their toddlers. The difference is in how Ethan internalized those actions. He got into a pattern and didn't get the part about that pattern only being appropriate in certain circumstances.

"Now, if we're not careful, we'll send him a different message - one that says we don't trust you. You're not like other kids. You can't handle yourself. You must have an adult glued to your side."

"If that's what it takes to keep him safe."

"Sara, there is another way, several other ways in fact, but they're not fast. Look. Here's another worry I have. The playground is an important social arena for kids. They learn a lot out there and practice much-needed skills like negotiation, compromise, cooperation, turn-taking and fair play. But kids won't play with that one child who has an adult beside him. A one-to-one aide would isolate Ethan. Not only would we be sending him the message that we don't trust him and don't believe he can learn to be like other kids, but we're sending that same message to every other student on the playground. It would be like pasting a big 'Don't Play With Me' sign onto Ethan's forehead. He'd be one kid standing alone with an adult while all the other children raced around and had fun without him."

Rob could tell by Sara's expression that she could envision this happening to her son.

"But he's not a bad boy. He just doesn't know. I want him to have friends. I want him to play with other kids just like any other little boy."

Rob pushed the tissue box closer to Sara once again. "Then we're on the same page. We both want the same things for Ethan. And, I, for one, believe that he can learn not to run away. There are certain ways kids comport themselves in schools and out in the public. Ethan can learn these ways. How about it? Are you up for working with me on this?"

Chapter 13

Rob pulled a piece of paper towards himself. "I'm a visual thinker and need to see, not just talk about it when I make a plan. Now, how should we start? Any ideas?"

Sara looked blank, so Rob suggested, "What about using an ABC to map it out?" When Sara still looked blank, he drew one horizontal line near the top of the page and created three vertical columns. At the top of the first column he wrote Antecedent. The middle column was titled Behavior and the last one Consequences. "Now, think of a time when Ethan ran. What was happening before? This might give us a clue as to why he ran."

"The last time I know about was last week at home. We were having company over, my husband's boss and his wife. Ethan had never met them before and I didn't know them very well either. He was pretty good while I was cooking and getting ready, but the Jacksons had only been at our house about ten minutes when we heard a thump, the door slammed and Ethan was gone."

"What was happening about the time he ran?"

"I'm not sure. The only people in that room were Nona Jackson and Ethan. She was very distressed and said she was just trying to lift Ethan onto her knee to read him a story. She reached for him and when she tried to cuddle him he went like a limp noodle and fell through her lap to the floor. She's positive he wasn't hurt but said he got up off the floor and ran."

"Was there anything about her you can identify that might have bothered Ethan?"

"She had on this frilly, starchy blouse that made scratchy sounds when she moved. I remember thinking it looked like those old, starched collars and must be awfully uncomfortable.

"Anything else?"

"She had on perfume. Not that cheap cologne, but obviously good quality scent. She must have really liked it because she wore a lot of it. A lot. When she entered the house, it was almost overpowering and made me wonder what the interior of their car must smell like."

"Ethan's not used to perfume?"

"No. When he was a toddler, he had eczema and we had to use scent-free detergents and soaps. Since scents bothered Ethan, I never wore perfume. His eczema's all gone now, but I never got back into the habit of wearing perfume. We don't light scented candles and those sorts of things either. We stopped, and then just never started again."

"Let's go on to 'B' for a minute and describe the behavior. What exactly did Ethan do?"

"I'm not positive since all I have is Mrs. Jackson's word for it. According to her, everything was fine although she was having some trouble lifting Ethan onto her knee. She said he was all stiff. She thought he'd warm up once she cuddled him and started reading."

"What happened next?"

"She said that he then made himself go limp and dropped to the floor. The sound we heard was his legs hitting the floor. Then he got up and ran for the front door. We heard it slam, then Ethan was gone."

"Where did he go?"

"Across the lawn and then down the sidewalk. My husband caught him pretty quickly."

"What did he do when he caught him?"

"He picked him up and carried him the way Ethan likes it - like a monkey. You know, chest to chest, Ethan's arms and legs clinging tight and his dad's arms around him. He's always liked this. He puts his head on your shoulder and relaxes."

"Okay. Let's go back a minute to 'A', the Antecedent. What do you think precipitated the running?"

"It could have been anything - the perfume, a strange woman trying to hold him, the stiff rustling of her blouse, unexpectedly having other people in our house, or anything else. Who knows?"

"Unexpected company?"

"Well, obviously I knew they were coming and we prepared the meal but I don't think we told Ethan until the doorbell rang and they were here."

"Sounds like any one of those things could have upset Ethan then a couple piled on top of each other might have felt like too much and he needed to escape."

Sara nodded.

Rob pointed to the last column. "And what was the consequence to all this?"

"The main consequence was that it spoiled our evening. I stayed with Ethan up in his room while my husband tried to entertain our guests on his own. It was not the best evening for anyone."

"Anyone?"

"No, none of us had a good time."

"What about Ethan? What kind of a time did he have after the two of you retreated to his bedroom?"

"Oh, Ethan was fine, probably better than any of us. We watched a couple of his favorite videos, I read him a story, and we played with his Lego, that sort of stuff."

"Does he like having your attention all to himself?"

"Sure. What kid doesn't?"

"So what was the negative consequence to Ethan for running away?"

Sara hesitated. "Well, he got frightened. Is that what you mean?"

"Not exactly. I mean what was the consequence he went through for having chosen running as his means of getting out of a situation he didn't like?"

"None, I don't think."

"Maybe this isn't a good example. What consequence does he receive at other times when he runs away?"

"I'm not sure what you mean."

"Say you're out shopping and he doesn't stay with you in a mall. What consequence do you impose on him later? Some people might think of it as a punishment if you like that word better."

"We don't really do things like that. I don't generally spank him and I certainly wouldn't spank a child who was frightened."

"Spanking isn't quite what I had in mind. I'll try to explain what I mean. There is a consequence for all our actions. Some consequences are good - we like them and they get us what we want. Other consequences we don't find so pleasant, especially the consequences we experience after making a bad decision. Those are the kinds of consequences I'm talking about. What kind have you found are effective with Ethan?"

Still, Sara hesitated, so Rob gave her some examples.

"Do you give him a time out, send him to his room, remove a toy, not let him watch television, make him go to bed early? The kind of consequences parents often use to teach lessons to their child."

"You have to understand. Ethan is different. He's been difficult from the start, but then later, we learned that he has autism. The diagnosis explains some of the difficulties he's always had but we're of course saddened by it. And we feel sorry for our poor little boy."

"I understand all that. But," he tapped his pen on the paper under the 'C' column, "for our purposes now, we need to see what the consequences are of his actions."

Silence from Sara.

"Are we in agreement that running away is a bad thing, something we want stopped?"

"Yes, of course."

"And you're with me on finding ways to teach Ethan not to run away but to find other ways of handling the situations?"

"Yes," a bit more hesitantly.

"Well, in order to teach him effective choice-making, he's going to have to experience consequences – both good consequences and ones he doesn't like. Just like all of us. We're rewarded for making good choices and things don't go as we'd like when we make poor choices."

Rob grabbed a second piece of paper. "Tell me what Ethan enjoys." He began writing the favorite activities Sara listed.

She asked, "Why do you want to know those things?"

"So we can give him appropriate rewards whenever he makes good choices."

"I thought a minute ago you were talking about punishments."

"I like to start with the positive. It's easier to give a child a positive consequence for making a good decision than giving a negative one for a poor choice. It's easier to get a kid to buy in to a plan when he likes the rewards he's working towards."

Rob put down his pen and looked at Sara. "I can try to do this alone here at school. That's not the best way, not by far, but I could do it. The downside to that would be what Ethan learns. I've seen many kids who learn to follow the rules and to make good choices at school but don't carry over the same skills at home. They seem to sense that the two environments are different and that the same rules don't apply.

"For Ethan's sake, it would be ideal if we worked on this together - you, your husband and me as well as the other staff at this school. If we surround Ethan, with everyone giving the same message, I'm positive we can at least seriously decrease his running away, if not make it disappear altogether. But to do this, we all need to agree to give pleasurable consequences when he does the right thing and consequences he won't like if he's run away."

"Are you asking me to be mean to my only son?"

"No, no, not at all. This is teaching him, just as you teach any other skill."

"Then are you telling me to bribe my own kid into being good?"

"Nope. That's not what I mean either. Look on the night you had the Jacksons over, Ethan likely felt overwhelmed by both the unexpectedness of those people dropping in and by sensory sensations. He ran away. That's a bad thing. Granted, Ethan was trying to get away from something he didn't like, but there are other ways he could have accomplished that. Safer ways and I think that's what you want. It's certainly what I want for him, both here at school and at home. As far as I can see, this is a crucial life skill, one he needs to learn for his own safety, to say nothing of his parents' peace of mind."

"We would feel a lot better if we weren't constantly in fear that he might run and get hurt or lost" Sara admitted.

"Let's get back to consequences. That evening at your place, how do you think Ethan felt when his dad carried him home?"

"Relieved. You could see it in his face. Relieved and relaxed. And he had fun. As they got closer to the house, Rick started jostling Ethan up and down. It's a game they play and by the time they got in the house, they were both laughing."

"From Ethan's point of view, how do you think this whole thing turned out?"

"He got scared, and then he wasn't?" Sara's statement was a question. She wasn't getting it. Rob was not doing a good enough job of explaining his point.

"Here's what I think went on in your son's mind. He was startled by the disruption to his routine when these strangers came over unexpectedly. He had no preparation for this."

"We don't exactly need our child's permission to invite guests over!"

"Of course not. But Ethan is the kind of kid who needs to know when things are going to happen that are different or unexpected. All it requires is a sentence or two. Or, grab a pencil and a scrap of paper and jot down a quick social story about having company. Anything will do, just so long as he has some warning, even a five minute warning might have helped."

Rob continued. "Then these strangers arrived. One tried to touch him in ways he didn't like. Some people approach little kids with a gentle touch, one they think will be soothing to a child. But to kids with tactile sensitivities, that soft touch will grate on their nerves and might even be perceived as hurtful. A firmer touch would likely have been a better approach. Mrs. Jackson told you it was hard to get Ethan on her knee because he was stiff as a board."

"Yes, that's what she said."

"So, in nonverbal language, Ethan was resisting. He did not want to sit on her knee. But this woman didn't know him so didn't read his body language. Of course, it might have helped if Ethan had used his words."

"Yes, but he might have said something rude or offended the wife of my husband's boss."

"We don't want him being rude, but would a couple rude words have made the situation any worse than his running off did?"

Sara shook her head.

"So, Ethan doesn't like this lady or being touched by her, so he runs away. By running, he escapes the smells or touches he didn't like about that woman. So, that's a positive consequence for him, don't you agree?"

"Yes, I suppose so."

"When he runs, he probably doesn't experience near the fear that you and your husband go through. He's a little boy, not thinking about all the things that could possibly happen to him. In this particular case, his running was positively reinforced as a good thing because it got him away from that strange woman."

"I guess it did."

"Then when your husband went after him, Ethan got to ride home in his favorite position. That position conjures up fun in his mind because it's a way to play with his dad. He got to be held tightly, giving good proprioceptive feedback to his body, something he was probably craving. Again, this is a positive consequence for having run. Then, and probably best of all, he got to spend a lovely evening with his mom, doing all the things he enjoys and he had your attention all to himself. How could running away be a bad thing?"

"When you put it that way, I can't see any reason for him to not run the next time."

"Exactly. That's why we have to break this pattern and give him new tools to get what he wants, more appropriate tools that will keep him safe."

"Back to this incident with the Jacksons. I wonder, and this is just a suggestion. Do you think in future it might be a good idea to not leave Ethan alone with a stranger until they have gotten used to each other?"

"You're right, so right. This is all my fault."

"We're not talking about faults here. That does not enter into it at all. What we're doing is making a plan to help Ethan be more successful the next time he runs into an unpleasant situation."

"What do you want us to do?"

"Glad you asked." He flashed her a grin. "Homework for Mr. and Mrs. Fellows. You know your son well and he talks to you more than to anyone else. Make up a list of ways Ethan can politely tell people to leave him alone the next time he finds himself in a similar situation. Could he ask to go to his room? Could he say that he wants to play by himself for a while now? I don't know but you and Mr. Fellows will come up with ideas that work best for your family."

"We can do that."

"Next, from that list, pick the items that you think would work here at school and give the list to me. We'll work on using the same words you're using at home, reinforcing each other."

"Makes sense to me." Sara was starting to feel more upbeat about this planning business.

"Last, please give me two other lists - one of consequences Ethan would think of as rewards, things I can use when he shows good decision-making. Plus, I need a list of consequences he won't like, ones to be used when he makes a bad choice. These might consist of the removal of something he likes. Can you do that?"

Sara nodded but without enthusiasm.

"Do you think we're on the right track?"

"Mostly. It's just that it will break my heart to be mean to my little boy."

"You know Sara, I look at it the opposite way. I see it as being mean to not curb this behavior and to not teach him better ways of responding to unpleasant situations. I'd feel mean if Ethan ran and got hurt. It would have been cruel to do nothing to prevent that. Try as we might we can't always be with him - not you, not his dad and not anyone at school. There will be times when Ethan must make a wise choice all on his own. Now is the time to help guide him so that he learns those skills."

Chapter 14

Ellie glanced out the bakery window. Rob Sells was coming down the street. Wiping her floury hands on her apron, she strode out the door and across the street towards him. "So, you were shining me on." Ellie's hands clenched, her lips were tight and she leaned her face in towards Rob's. He thought she might spit the words at him.

Rob took a step back.

"What's the matter with you?"

"Nothing's wrong with me except I'm ticked at the indifference one human being can show to another, especially you."

"I don't know what's got your panties in a knot but you're looking at the wrong guy. I haven't even seen you in over a week. Whatever's happened to you, it wasn't me. So, back off." His hands went into his back pockets.

"Who said it was all about me? Some of us care about others too, especially those who can't defend themselves."

Rob was torn between wanting to walk away and learning what had changed the softer Ellie of the other night back into the shrew he'd first met. Ah, it wasn't worth it. "I'm out of here." Rob turned to walk away, back in the opposite direction from the bakery.

Ellie snagged his left arm as he turned. Rob looked pointedly down at her hand, then up at her face, but she didn't let go. "Not so fast, mister," she told him. "Not until I find out why you're not doing your job as a teacher."

"Are you out of your friggin' mind?" Then he added, "Get your hand away from my arm. I have things to do." Rob glanced around to see if other people were observing the scene they were making.

Ellie didn't budge, nor did she look around. "You know, the other night

I thought I'd been wrong about you, that you actually were a nice guy - running a boys' group, trying to learn so you could help those kids. On our walk home I was even starting to get some warm and fuzzy thoughts about you."

This gave Rob pause. "You were?"

"Forget that. I was wrong. I can be such an idiot some times."

"Can't say I've noticed," the sarcasm thick in his voice.

She gave his arm a shake. "So why are you refusing to help Sara?"

"How is my teaching or my student's mother any business of yours?"

Ellie's shoulder's drooped. "Once I had this friend. She needed someone to stand up for her and no one did. She killed herself." She looked up at Rob with defiance. "That's never going to happen to someone I know again."

Relaxing his stance just a bit, Rob turned back toward this quieter Ellie. "Why don't you start at the beginning and tell me what I'm supposed to have done or not done."

"Sara can't have a life. She spends every moment of her day by a phone, waiting for a call from the school."

"Did she tell you how often I've called her during the school day?"

"No, not exactly, but obviously enough times to keep her on the edge of her seat waiting for the next call. She's just so sad."

"Her being sad is my fault too?"

"Maybe for some of it. I didn't go into all the details of her life but I know that school stuff is a big part of it."

"You might want to check how much of this happens now and how much was at their previous school."

That gave Ellie momentary pause, but she carried on. "Here's what she says. She's overwhelmed. She loves her kid, but he's difficult. I know what she means, having seen some of what Ben's been through with Kyle. While Kyle's fits of screaming have lessened a lot over the past year, it does not sound like Ethan's are getting any better.

"Did you stop to think of why Kyle seems better?"

"Well, it's Mel of course. And a bit my brother. He might be a lug but he tries. When Ben learned how to do things differently, Kyle reacted by screaming less."

"So you're saying that the adults in Kyle's life helped him learn a different way of coping?"

"Something like that, I guess. Sara needs the same kind of help Ben got."

"You're saying Sara needs to marry Mel?" Rob tried to lighten things up a bit.

Ellie jabbed his side with her elbow. "She needs the help of someone like Mel, someone who knows kids with autism. You're his teacher.

Couldn't you be a help instead of being the ogre who's adding to the stress?"

Rob shook his head at her. "I can't talk to you about Ethan or Sara. I can talk in generalities about autism and parenting." He continued, "Parenting any kid is not a cake walk but it's especially hard when your child has autism. Some of the instinctual, parenting things won't work in the same way they would with a typical kid. So, you have to learn different ways, different strategies. Is it harder? Definitely. It takes more patience, more repetitions, more time."

"Such as?"

"Has Mel talked to you about Kyle and auditory processing?"

"Yeah, I get some of it."

"How would you explain it to Sara?"

"Well, most of us are talkers. And, the more frustrated or tired or angry we get, the more we talk to kids. We lecture. We threaten. We cajole. We talk, talk, talk."

"And all that goes over the head of a kid with autism."

"Mel keeps telling us that talking can make things worse. The kid is already upset, unsure what to do and how to avoid the things that are bothering him. Then Ben would loom over him, yammering away, his voice getting louder, but the words made no sense to Kyle. This just increased Kyle's tension and then he'd blow."

"Mel was right to be worried. The problem with a kid getting in the habit of blowing is that he gets bigger and the tantrums turn to aggression. The longer the pattern continues, the more entrenched it becomes. A two year old may throw his cup or a stuffed toy. An older kid may overturn a desk or throw dishes at you. Someone could and will get hurt."

"I think that's happening to Sara now. She was crying when she showed me the bruise on her forehead from some toy Ethan hit her with. She says it makes her afraid to go near her own child when he's upset, even when she knows he needs a hug."

That gave Rob pause. "I'm sorry to hear it's gone that far with them." They were both silent a moment.

"So what happens now?" Ellie asked. "Does it just get worse and worse, a parent held hostage by her own kid?"

"It can go that way. Except for rare cases, it doesn't have to be like that. You can turn it around, although the younger you start, the easier it is."

"How? What can she do?"

"Think back to the things that Ben learned to do with Kyle. Name one thing he does that you might not see in other households."

Ellie was quick to answer. "Visuals. I'd never heard the term before and certainly never seen them plastered all over a house like that. But once Ben started using them and once Kyle caught on, it did make a difference. Kyle wouldn't be screaming and Ben wouldn't be yelling and exasperated. Well, he didn't actually yell all that much, but he certainly felt like it. I could tell. And believe you me, my brother can yell. You try being his little sister and get into his precious stuff when we were kids."

Rob smiled. "I can imagine you doing that quite often."

"He was older and had interesting stuff. It was especially intriguing since I wasn't supposed to be in his room."

"I bet you were a real brat."

"If you listened to Ben, yes. But I'm quite sure he has that all wrong."

"Tell me more about the visuals that Ben learned to use."

"To begin with Ben was late for work every day and late getting Kyle to school. Ben absolutely detests being late for anything and he's usually an organized guy, but no matter how early he started in the morning, he could not get Kyle up and ready on time.

"Then Mel helped him make these pictures of what Kyle was supposed to do in the morning. It took a bit of time, but not long before Kyle understood what each picture stood for and then he followed them in order. When he'd get sidetracked and start to play with his Lego™ or watch a Dora the Explorer™ movie, instead of raising his voice and ragging on Kyle, Ben would tap on the picture strip and show Kyle. And, believe it or not, Kyle would follow what the picture said. It wasn't perfect, but they didn't end up leaving the house mad at each other and they mostly got going on time."

"Good. What else did Ben do?"

"I guess the other biggie was social stories. He learned that from Mel, too. At first Ben couldn't believe that they worked because instead of words, Mel often drew pictures of what was going to happen. She really cannot draw. Did you know that? Ben would look at what she'd made and not have a clue what it was supposed to be. Mel said it didn't matter. She'd tell Kyle what it was about and he'd believe her. Then they'd follow the pictures and it would be all right. Well, maybe not totally all right, but at least far better than it used to be. You should have seen the ruckus Kyle made originally when he had to go in the elevator. But the social story helped."

"Yeah, elevators can be scary places for some kids. They're small, enclosed spaces. The door closes and you can feel trapped inside. Then this little box you're in makes strange clankings and whirrings and then it starts to move. You're not used to feeling the ground beneath your feet rattle or move. For a kid with no sense of time, it could feel like being trapped forever and he'd have no idea when it would be over, if ever. Anyone with vestibular problems, unsure of their balance or where their body is in space would be disoriented in that moving box.

"Did Kyle ever get over his fear?"

"Not perfectly, but it got better and better. So much better in fact that one night he took off on his own and they lost him for a couple hours. Ben almost went out of his mind."

"What happened?"

"Kyle for some reason went to Mel's house. It was quite a walk for a little guy and it was night time. No one had any idea he even knew the way. He would have had to go through the park in the dark, and then a couple blocks the other side. They found him asleep on Mel's deck with her dog curled around him."

"Scary stuff. Has it only happened that once?"

"Yes. Kyle's never shown any want to go off on his own again. But then Mel and her dog now live with them so there's no need to go find them. I actually think the whole thing was more traumatic for Ben than for Kyle. My brother was a wreck."

They were silent for a moment.

"Hey, did you notice something?" Ellie asked.

Rob sighed. "What now? Have you found another way in which I'm evil incarnate?"

Ellie pretended to whack Rob's arm. "I was about to ask if you've noticed that we're not fighting anymore. But maybe we should revert back. That seems to be our default mode."

"Fighting? Me? Look lady, you're the one who attacked me. I was on my way for some good coffee, maybe something sweet and I'd had the faint hope of some pleasant conversation. Guess I was wrong on all accounts, especially the latter."

It was Ellie's turn to sigh. Her eyes remained on the toes of Rob's sneakers. "Look, I'm sorry. Ben's always telling me that I run too hot and I blow off without getting all the facts.

"But this time I really thought I did have all the facts. If you could have seen Sara yesterday, you'd know what I mean. It's not everyday someone comes into my bakery and cries. Actually, I can only think of it happening twice in the past year and both times it was Sara doing the crying. I don't think she has many friends and comes to me for a sympathetic ear."

"And what does your sympathetic ear tell your mouth to say to her?"

"She's obviously hurting and she needs someone to stand up for her."

"And you've appointed yourself guardian of sad mothers?"

"Are you saying there's something wrong with helping someone in need?"

"Nah." His face softened. "I don't know if I could tell you to quit it, even if I wanted to. It seems to be part of who you are."

Now Ellie looked uncomfortable. "Maybe because I was raised in a house with three brothers, I can't stand to see someone being picked on."

Rob bristled again. "For the last time, I am not picking on anyone and that includes Sara and her son. Geez. Get off it, will ya?"

"I didn't mean you, at least not this time anyway. It's just that in general I can't stand bullies."

"Bullies! Now you're calling me a bully. As I said before, you, lady are a piece of work." He turned to walk away but didn't get far. Ellie still had hold of his arm. "Do you mind?" he asked, looking down at her hand restraining his arm.

"Actually, I do. It's hard to hold a conversation with you when you keep trying to walk away."

"My attempts to walk away should send a message to you. What about it don't you get?"

"I know you're not really trying to get away."

"Short of creating a scene in public, yeah, I am trying to get away. In case you hadn't noticed, this is not my idea of a good time on my day off."

"Come off it. Anytime you wanted, you could have pulled away from me."

"Yeah? Says who?"

"Says me. Admit it, you like me."

He pulled back his head and looked at her. "I like the woman who accosts me every time I see her? The same one who accuses me of all manner of heinous crimes?"

Ellie nodded. Then she smiled and Rob's body slumped. How could you stay mad at a being like Ellie? He returned her smile. "Maybe I do, just a little."

Her smile broadened even more. She tugged on his arm. "Come on. I'll buy you a coffee. I know a nice little place not far from here." They set off together for the bakery, Ellie chatting and Rob wondering how he had gotten himself into this.

Chapter 15

"I don't get it," said Ellie. "What is about people like Mel that make it look easy to raise a child who has autism?"

"Easy? I doubt that Mel would say that, or anybody else. I imagine that Mel finds it a bit harder now that she's a mother. Before, she was just a teacher and that made it easier. You can go home at the end of the day and concentrate on other things, although your students are always in the back of your mind.

"Someone like Mel has extra training in strategies for kids with special needs and for behavior issues. That was the focus of the graduate work that we both did. Still, you only learn so much from books and the real knowledge you gain is from the classroom, working with the kids and with their parents. Those two groups are the best teachers."

"That's fine for people like you and Mel who have the time to go back to school for this training. But what's the average parent to do?"

"People like Mel and I?" He was back to bristling, something Ellie brought out in him more than any other person had ever done. "When we did our Master's degrees, we had full-time jobs. We studied evenings and weekends and spent our vacation time sitting in lecture theaters. Every spare penny we could gather went into tuition and books."

"So why'd you do it?"

"To get better at our jobs. To learn more about what makes kids tick, especially kids who learn in different ways."

"And did you get better?"

"I like to think so. Yes, I'm pretty sure I did, at least for the most part. I get these kids in the fall and by spring they've grown physically, but also mentally and emotionally. They're more in control of themselves, they've acquired more social skills and they've come along academically. Not all of them progress at the same pace or in the same areas, but I have to admit that they all do make progress. So yes, I do think I'm a success when you look at those measurements."

"But a parent wouldn't have this fund of knowledge that you and Mel acquired. What can they do?"

"The knowledge about strategies and things to try is out there. You don't have to read ominous textbook tomes to get it, either. In fact, we have a lending library of such resources at school, available for any parent."

"Why don't some take advantage of it and why is this all so hard for Sara."

"Sara is the parent of one of my students," he reminded her. "I cannot talk about any of my kids or their families with you. Does that sound familiar, ring a bell with you somewhere?"

"All right, I get it. Don't talk about her, just about parents in general."

"Remember, these things are just my opinions. I think that for parents, there is some guilt."

"What do you mean guilt? It's not like they purposely gave their child autism!"

"No, of course not. Guilt does not have to be logical, does it? Whether or not it makes sense, there is some guilt about things like, What if I did something wrong that caused this? Did I expose myself to some toxin that got into the baby? Did I have too many x-rays? Or not enough prenatal tests? I had a lot of late nights during my first trimester. Did that stress the baby too much? I had one beer before I even knew I was pregnant. Or, is it my genes? Some people spend hours going through their family genealogy trying to find signs of autism in one family or the other so they can blame the other spouse's genetic line."

"Are they right? Did they do something to cause this in their child?"

"Maybe but most likely not. The cause of autism spectrum disorders is still not known. They've found over three dozen genes that might be implicated in autism but twin studies find some of those genes in both twins, but one has autism and the other doesn't.

"Then, we've all known of mothers who truly did not look after themselves during pregnancy and that baby is not born with any evidence of autism."

"So, accurate or not, some parents might blame themselves for their child having autism."

"Yes, autism or any other problem. Then there's the way people react to that guilt. Some feel that they have to make it up to their child. They see their kid suffering and they want that to stop so they cater to his every whim, trying to apologize for what they perceive as the hard life he leads."

"I can see that. I'd do the same thing."

"It certainly is tempting, but there's another way to look at it. For the child, this is the only life he's ever known. Unless someone tells him, he's not even aware when he's young that things are harder for him than for others his age. To him, things just are. I'm not convinced that feeling sorry for a kid does him any good. Sure, as adults we might feel badly watching him struggle, but keep that to yourself - that's your issue, not the kid's. Feeling sorry for him conveys the message that something is wrong with him, that he's a thing to be pitied. That's not good for anyone."

"Isn't that a little harsh?"

"Well, maybe. I don't mean it quite that way, but feeling sorry for a child doesn't help him. Yes, that kid will have struggles, ones that his peers don't have and some that they do. Rather than feeling sorry for him and indulging him to compensate, I believe you should spend your time equipping that kid with the tools he's going to need to manage his life. There. That's my soapbox for the afternoon."

Ellie sat back in her chair and clapped her hands. "And a fine one it is. I couldn't have done better myself. But is that it? Do you have any more thoughts on this?"

"Thought you'd never ask. Okay, just like when grief can take different forms when someone close to you dies, there is a grief process when the baby you'd anticipated didn't turn out exactly as you'd imagined. We all have this dream of an angelic cherub nestled into our arms, smiling and responsive to our touch. But many kids with autism aren't like that. The initial parent-child bonding can be tough when the baby doesn't seem to respond to your gestures, when he doesn't gaze into your eyes, or relish your cuddling. Some kids with autism scream a lot, sort of like a baby with colic that lasts for years. In those situations, it must be hard not to resent that child at times with all the effort you're putting in being rewarded with still more screams. Then, you'd feel guilty for resenting your own child, especially when the kid is obviously in distress or he wouldn't be howling. So there's guilt over having a child with a problem and guilt over resenting all the care it takes to look after this kid. Guilt can be paralyzing."

A waitress stopped by their table with a pot in her hand. "More coffee," she offered.

Ellie waited for Rob's response. "Thanks, but I'm all coffee'd out now."

"None for me either, Kim." She looked at her watch, then around the bakery. She saw that there were no customers left, the baked goods had been put away and the coffee machines dismantled and rinsed. "Sorry. The time got away on me. But I see that you have everything under control. Go grab any of the left-over baking that you'd like to take home and please tell the others to do the same. Thanks for tidying up; I appreciate it. Only, next time, yell for me. Don't let me be such a slacker."

"You? A slacker? That'd be the day. But, thanks and yeah we'd love to grab some of your baking. Night."

"What about you?" Ellie looked at Rob. "Hungry?"

"A bit, but not for anything sweet. I think my stomach's saying protein is needed. I think I have a couple steaks in the freezer that I could grill. Care to come over and sample my cooking?"

"See, you do like me."

"Not particularly. It's just that I don't get that many opportunities to sound off on my favorite subjects. You asked, so I had a captive audience. I'm not finished, way not finished so I don't want to lose my listener. And if you're going to have to listen for the next hour, I suppose I have to feed you."

"When you put it that way, how could a gal refuse?"

Chapter 16

"This is cute." Ellie looked around the yard.

"Cute?" Rob asked. Just what a guy wants to hear about his place.

"Seriously, it is cute. Cute in a nice, manly way."

"Hah, that's better. I rent the main floor and this patio comes with it. There's a suite in the basement, one above me and a tiny one in the attic space. We're all either grad students or working people so it's pretty quiet." They were stretched out on matching chaise lounges. Every once in a while Rob would get up to turn over the baking potatoes and the corn on the cob. "Almost time for the steaks."

"I love a man who can cook."

Rob raised one eyebrow at her. "What's that supposed to mean?"

"Nothing. I just love it when a man can cook."

"So I do have some redeeming charms after all."

"Actually you have many, well probably, but I haven't had enough time yet to dig deep enough to find them all."

"Have I just been insulted or complimented?"

"Neither. Both. But you are intriguing enough that I'll have to take the time to do that digging."

"Again, I can't tell if that's a threat or a promise."

"Settle on the fact that you're an interesting guy." Before Rob could think more about that, she told him, "Tell me more. I want to know about this parenting and autism stuff."

"Okay. There's the guilt stuff that we talked about but on top of all that is the fatigue. All parents of young kids are exhausted, from the baby stage on up. It takes a lot of time and energy to raise a child. But when that child has autism, the demands are far, far greater and so is the energy required."

"What do you mean?"

"Take sleep for instance. Most babies sleep through the night before their first birthday. A child with autism may not do that until they're almost ready for school. Some sleep very little, just cat naps here and there. And when an overactive baby or toddler is awake, a parent must also be awake to oversee what's happening. Sleep is often an issue throughout the life of a person with autism, but when you have a sleep-deprived child, you also have a sleep-deprived parent. Think about how you function when you've had a number of late nights in a row. Probably you're not at your best, your problem-solving skills go down, and your frustration level rises. Now think about feeling that way all the time and pile that on top of the guilt we talked about earlier. How well would you stay one step ahead of your kid? How much time could you devote to studying about autism and mapping out careful plans? Yes, that is exactly what such a parent should do but often they're simply hanging on by their toenails and have no time to even sit and reflect."

"That sounds like how Ben was when he first got Kyle. And he got his son because Kyle's mother said she couldn't take it anymore and could no longer look after him."

"What did Ben do?"

"Took him, of course. What did you think he'd do?"

"Sorry. Geez, you're prickly. Your brother seems to be doing a good job with him now."

"Yeah, now he is. But it was pretty rough at first, rough on both Ben and on Kyle."

"So, what else is going on with parents?"

"They hunker down. When you feel that you're at the end of your rope, you're exhausted and there's no end in sight, you hunker down. You put one foot in front of the other as best you can, just to survive. There's no time or energy left to stand back and reflect or to contemplate doing things differently. Often people get caught in this loop. They try the same things over and over again, but those things aren't working for either the kid or for the parents."

"That's like, 'If you do what you've always done, you'll get what you've always got.' Who said that anyway?"

"Not sure. Was it Henry Ford? No, wait. It might have been Mark Twain. Dunno. But it always reminds me of this other quote - 'If you want to change the result, you must change the way you do things'. I have no idea who said that one, but I like it."

"But based on what you've said, these parents are too busy surviving to think about how to change things," said Ellie.

"Plus, making radical changes means admitting that what you were doing before wasn't good enough. Most of us have enough ego that it's hard to admit that we've been wrong or that we don't have the answers."

"That's hardly fair. What these parents are likely doing are the same things most parents do or that they watched their own parents doing. And, usually it all works out pretty well."

"Exactly. But raising a kid who is on the autism spectrum takes more. The normal stuff might not work or not be enough."

"I still say that's not fair," Ellie protested.

"Who said anything about fair? Is it fair for Kyle that he has to work harder than most kids to stay calm and regulated during the school day? Is it fair that his sensory system launches into overdrive at the slightest provocation? Nope, none of it is fair. But it is what it is."

"Sort of play the hand you're dealt, eh?"

"Yep. Feeling sorry for him or doing any of that woe-is-me stuff does not help Kyle or any other kid in his situation. All that is actually more about the parents and how they feel than about their child."

For a while, their mouths were too full of steak and corn to talk much. Butter dripped down both their chins. Rob liked that Ellie didn't seem to care - she actually laughed at herself. When his cob of corn almost rolled off his plate, she yelled, "Three second rule", but he caught it before it hit the grass, sparing him from deciding if the rule that anything on the ground less than three seconds was still okay to eat should apply in this case.

Since Rob hadn't expected company, he only had one beer in the fridge, so they split it. They sat, quietly sipping from their glasses. Ellie remarked on what a beautiful evening it had turned out to be.

Rob sprang to his feet. "Evening. Evening! Shit! I forgot. This is the evening of our support group, the first night for this session." He glanced at his watch. "It starts in half an hour. Sorry, but I gotta run. He noticed the butter stains and the odd steak dripping on his shirt and swiftly pulled it over his head as he ran into the house. "Don't think you have to leave. Stay, stay and relax." His voice was muffled for a moment, and then his head popped out of a clean golf shirt. He heard the water running in the kitchen sink as Ellie began washing their dishes. "Just leave that stuff. I'll get it later. You don't have to clean up." Although his words said the right things, he was relieved to have her help. And he was pleased that she would even think of pitching in in this way. The woman he'd briefly dated a few months ago would never have considered risking her French manicure in dish water. Ellie was fun and low maintenance and relaxing to be around. Too relaxing. He had almost missed this meeting because he was enjoying his time with her too much.

"What's this important meeting about?" Ellie asked.

"It's a parent support group Mel and I run each semester. Tonight's the first meeting for this group."

"Parents, huh? Isn't it a little strange that you have no kids and Mel just acquired one, yet the two of you run a parent support group?

"It's not just parents. Hey, why don't you come along? There are grandparents and other relatives who attend, not just parents. Everyone who comes is concerned about a child who is struggling in some way. You see Kyle a lot; maybe you'd even learn something. Or, share with the group things you've found that work with your nephew."

Ellie looked skeptical.

"It's up to you. It's at the school at seven o'clock and only lasts an hour or so. Honestly, you're welcome. I know Mel would love for you to join us." Then, he was off.

Chapter 17

As the group took their seats, Rob noticed the empty chairs left between most people. Only those who came as a couple sat beside one another. By the third session, Rob knew that there would be no blank chairs, that the participants would have come together as a group and formed friendships. They'd shove the empty chairs out of the circle on their own and join ranks, literally and figuratively. It happened that way every time.

"Welcome," he began and introduced himself and Mel as the coordinators of the group. "Next, I want you all to introduce yourselves. If you want, just give your first name. Or, a first name, just something we can call you when you're in this room." That brought a polite chuckle. "If you want to tell us a bit more about yourself, that's fine too. Some people prefer to tell us that you're here because you're a parent to a child who has a specific challenge, but that's up to you. Give us a one word, one sentence or one paragraph introduction."

As usual, no one wanted to go first. Rob smiled encouragingly at one mother he'd met a number of times. She was about to speak when a voice spoke up from the back.

"I'm here because I've only recently gotten to know my nephew. He's a wonderful six year old. He has autism and I want to learn more about the things I can do to be a meaningful part of his life."

Ellie. Bless her, Rob thought. Yet another plus on the scorecard. He worried that the score was tallying far too high in his estimation. Yes, she could annoy the life out of him, but maybe putting up with some of that was worth the plusses he got from spending time with her. He reined in his thoughts as another woman spoke.

"We've recently become foster parents to three brothers diagnosed with fetal alcohol syndrome. We already love the boys but it's quickly become clear that we need help. We've fostered many kids before but we can tell that the things we normally do might not work this time."

Round the others went, some stating just a first name, others giving a glimpse into their history and the reason why they had sought out this group. The last to speak was Mel.

"I've run this group with Rob for the last few years. Never has it meant so much to me as it has this year. I got married last summer and am now the proud step-mother to an incredible little boy who happens to have autism. While I've taught kids with autism for many years now, it is different living with one. There's no turning out the lights and shutting the door at five o'clock anymore. I'm sure all of you know what I mean." The answering laughs showed that they did.

Rob took over. "First, I want to talk about the elephant in the room. We'll look at it, talk about it, then tell it to get lost.

"I imagine that every parent in this room shares the same thought - one you might not voice very often, but one that has haunted your thoughts. Here it is - 'It's my fault my child has these difficulties. I did something to cause this.' Now, I'm going to be blunt. No. No, whatever struggles your child has, they are not your fault. You are not to blame. You might have some power but I guarantee that you are not powerful enough to have caused this."

He paused and regarded each person, especially those who looked the most uncomfortable as if they were hiding their guilt. "Were you a perfect parent? Were you an exemplary mother while pregnant? Unlikely. But neither was your neighbor who has a child who has no disability. They made mistakes along the way, as did you. Whatever has happened to your child is not your fault. You didn't cause it to happen, you cannot fix it or make it go away. Are we clear on that?"

A number of people appeared unconvinced.

"None of that matters. What does matter is what we do from here on in. You can help your child. Life can get better for all of you. Not perfect, perhaps not totally typical, but better. I guarantee it and you must believe it possible too or you wouldn't be here tonight.

"By the way," he continued. "I know just what efforts you have gone to to make it here this evening. Mel and I will do our best to make this and every other meeting worth your while."

He glanced at Mel and she stepped forward. "Rob and I are not the experts - you are. While we've gone to school for extra training in working with kids with exceptional needs, you are the true experts of your individual children. You know them best. You've found things that work and don't work."

One fellow said, "You can say that again about the 'don't work' part."

Some of the tension left the room.

Mel continued. "Think about what it's like your first days on a new job. Then think about doing that same job six years down the road. You've learned a lot. Most of you have had at least that much experience with your child. While no two kids are alike, you can learn a lot from each other in this group. When you're pulling your hair out because nothing's working, someone else here might have found a solution to that problem and has moved on to their own new concern. There are twenty-four of us here tonight. Twenty-four times six means almost a century and a half of accumulated experience between us. Surely that counts for something if we just share what we've learned.

Rob said, "Sometimes people have looked to us as the experts. Yes, Mel and I are teachers, teachers who specialize in kids with learning differences. But, as you well know, we leave the building and go at the end of the afternoon and the kids come back to you. I might know how to cope with twenty some students during the day, but you know how to live with one special child all the time. I worry about them for a short span of the ten months they're in my room; you worry about them all the time. I send them home to you at three o'clock every day. On the other hand, all of you cheerfully send them back to me to have for six hours each day. You may have them one at a time at home with you, but I have them a couple dozen at a time."

He added, "Good thing we love them, isn't it?" The laughing was a bit louder and a trifle less forced this time.

"Now that we've talked about the fact that you are not to blame for your child having challenges, we'll move on to the next big item. Guilt. If you believe that you were somehow at fault, you'll feel guilt. In those more sane moments when you know that you could not possibly have caused this, you might still feel guilty. Why?"

"I love my daughter," a voice from the side of the room said. "But, sometimes I get sick of being on the same treadmill, the constant trips to the doctor's office, needing to get time off work, never any time to myself. Sometimes I resent the way my life has turned out since she's been born, then I kick my butt from here to China over feeling that way about my own flesh and blood. She can't help the way she is. She didn't ask to be born." Others nodded and added their assents. This seemed a common thread as others gave similar examples. The group was loosening up after realizing they were among like minds.

One woman said, "Sometimes I'm impatient with my son. He's so demanding and I'm so tired. I have a job and other kids and the house and everything. Some days it seems like too much, and then when my son needs something that messes up my plans, I lose it. Sometimes I yell at him. Then

I hate myself for doing that and try to make it up to him."

This was the opening Rob was waiting for. "You've made a good point," he told her. He addressed the whole group. "How many of you have felt impatient with your child then felt guilty and tried to make it up to him or her?"

Nearly every hand rose, including Rob's own. "We're human, so we make mistakes. Let's admit it and move on. But there is one part of this I'd like to talk about some more. From time to time we're all going to mess up, feel badly, and then move on. That's normal and our kids will forgive us. The problem comes when we can't get past the guilt and try to make it up with over-indulgence.

"We have more of an imagination than do kids. We can put ourselves in someone else's place and imagine how it must feel. We look at our children struggling and feel badly that life has handed them this path. So, maybe we try to be extra nice to the child. We buy things to make him happy. We let him have what he wants; we go out of our way to indulge him. Then, before you know it, you have on your hands a little tyrant. And the worst of it is, we've made him that way. Now, not only does our kid have some type of disability, but he's a brat as well."

The looks Rob was getting were no longer warm and fuzzy. "Yep," he continued, "I just called your little darling a brat. No, I don't mean necessarily that your particular offspring are brats, but can you see the possibility? That guilt could lead to spoiling a child?"

He waited. Many seemed unconvinced. "Trust me on this. Your son or daughter does not need you to feel sorry for him or her. They need your love and your care and your guidance, but not your pity. Pity won't help him learn the skills he needs to be as independent as he possibly can."

Rob felt the shift in the audience and realized he was coming on too strong. Time to tone it down a notch and take another tactic. He looked to Mel, but she was already stepping forward.

"What do you think the biggest impediment is to your child having a successful, independent life as an adult?" she asked.

"The fact that he has a diagnosis of autism," one dad said.

"His wheelchair," said another.

A mom offered, "Running away. He takes off the moment things aren't to his liking. He takes a year off my life every time he does that. At this rate, I'm not going to live to see him into his teenage years." A couple people laughed but several looked like they felt the same way.

"No," said Mel. "Well, at least not quite." She nodded at the mom what had just spoken. "Your example is likely closest."

So much for a gentler approach, thought Rob.

"Those things could be barriers but we can get around them. We'll learn and the kids can learn. The biggest barrier any one of your children will face is in not being able to manage themselves."

"What's that supposed to mean?" asked a woman in the front row. Several others nodded.

"It means being able to handle himself, more exactly, to calm himself when he's upset. To remain calm enough to think through his options when he encounters a problem. To react appropriately to the size of the problem."

"Well, my kid either throws something, yells or takes off when he runs into a problem."

"Yes, that might be what he does now, but we can turn that around," answered Mel.

The father looked skeptically at her. "Believe me, lady, we've tried. It's not as easy as just wishing it away."

"You're right. It's not easy. I absolutely agree," Mel told him. "But, it can be done."

Rob stepped in. "Look, it is human nature to fall into patterns. We all do it - that's how habits are formed. Anybody here ever tried to quit smoking?" Hands went up. "Well, you know it's hard and you don't lick it overnight. Our kids fall into habits as well. Maybe the first time or two that behavior got them what they wanted, whether that was an object, attention or they were trying to avoid something. So, a habit was formed. Whether or not that pattern of behaving fits every situation is another story, but kids don't often stop to analyze things in that way. Instead, they fall back on what they did the last time. And, if that behavior doesn't get them what they want, then they have to up the ante, increasing the behavior."

"How many of us have ever given in to a child's tantrum just to make him stop?" Mel answered her own question by raising her hand. Many of the parents joined her. "I'm not proud of it and in my ideal world, I'd never do such a thing again, but as Rob said, I'm human. My goal though, it to help kids not use those negative behaviors to control their world, but to find better, more appropriate ways to get what they want.

"Soon, we'll stop so you can stretch your legs. But, being a teacher, I have an assignment for you." Mel continued amid the groans. "This is your group. We want it to be helpful for you, worth your time and effort to make it here each week. There are a number of things we could focus on but we'd prefer to tailor these meetings to your needs.

"We're all here because we care about a child who is experiencing difficulties. Some of your kids share the same challenges. Talk to each other. See if you can find areas that worry several of you and we can focus on those issues."

"Like what?" someone asked.

"Some of the past groups have wanted to talk about things like getting a child to bed at night, getting everyone up and out of the house on time in the morning, hygiene, throwing things, tantrums, hiding, whatever seemed most pressing at the time."

Mel glanced at Rob. That was his cue to say, "Let's take a break for a few minutes. There's coffee and cookies at the table behind me."

"You're good," Ellie told Rob as she peered at him over the stiff, paper cup of coffee. "But you're coffee isn't."

"No one can make good coffee with a thirty cup percolator." He waited a second then asked, "You think I'm good?"

"Don't fish for compliments. You know that you are. There were a few times there when I thought the meeting was going south on you, but you pulled it back and got the audience to come with you."

"That part was mostly Mel's doing. We tag team pretty well and she's more of the sensitive type than I am."

"Mel! My Mel - sensitive? That truly is a hoot. I'd love to be there if Ben heard you say that. You should hear some of the stories he tells of how Mel treated him when they first met, when he was first learning how to manage things with Kyle. Mel had absolutely no patience with him." She giggled. "It was lovely to see. My big brother, the guy who's always so in control, always wants to be the boss, humbled by this little woman and obediently following her orders."

"He wouldn't have done that if her ideas didn't work, though."

"No, that's true. That's why he started to pay attention to her because when he tried even a few of her suggestions, it helped. And, believe me, he needed the help if he and Kyle were ever going to survive one another."

"They seem like a great family now."

"Oh, they are. Ben would move the earth for Kyle. At first this parenting thing started as a duty, his obligation. Then that kid wormed his way into Ben's heart and looking after him was no longer just something he was expected to do. It became his life."

"Yeah, kids can do that to you," Rob agreed.

Ellie looked at him curiously. "Why, do you have kids? Are you married? I never thought to ask that before."

Rob's brow furrowed as he looked down at her. "Don't you think that's something I might have mentioned? Do you think I stashed a wife in the hall closet when you came over for those steaks?"

"No, jeez, but some people are divorced, you know. You could have an ex-wife hanging around somewhere and maybe even a passel of kids."

"Passel?"

"You know what I mean. Just when I think you're an all right guy, you act like a jerk again."

"Does that mean you're about to start yelling at me again? Or yanking on my arm? Because if you are, how be you grab this one? My left one is still recovering from the bruises you gave me the last time."

Ellie's look of concern made him grin. She was reaching for his arm to check when she saw from his expression that he was kidding. "Jerk!" She punched his arm for emphasis. Rob rubbed that spot. "Now how am I going to mark papers tomorrow with an injured arm?"

"How'd we get into this anyway?"

"I think the conversation started with you telling me I'm good."

"Now, that was a mistake on my part."

"How so? Does the truth hurt?"

"God, talking to you is so hard."

"I don't see anyone forcing you to stand here." He gestured with his coffee cup toward the parents clustered in groups around the room. "There are plenty of other people here to talk to."

"Somehow, at the moment, I don't think they'd be as interesting."

"Interesting? Wow, first I'm good, and then I'm interesting. Things are working in my favor."

Ellie scrunched her nose at him. She so regretted giving this irritating man any sort of compliment.

Then he said, "You know, I find you interesting, too. In fact, very interesting."

That was not what she expected to hear. "Yeah?"

"Yeah. Interesting enough that I'd like to get to know you better. Can I buy you a coffee after the meeting's over?"

"That sounds delightful."

Chapter 18

Mel called the group back together. "I have a confession to make. My husband says I'm not known for being subtle. I have a tendency to say what I think. Unfortunately for you, so does Rob. For now though, you're stuck with us." She paused. "One advantage of this is that you'll get to know us, warts and all. We will be frank about what we think. We'll tell you about the mistakes we've made and how we've learned by trial and error. Some things we get right, others we haven't, but we try. And, we learn all the time. Sometimes we learn by studying but more often we learn from the kids and from parents like you. At times it may seem like we have a wealth of knowledge, and maybe we do, but we're lucky. We have the privilege of working with parents and teachers all the time so we can soak up their knowledge and share that with you."

Rob's turn. "Since we're planning to be open with you, we hope that you'll feel free to do the same with us. Most likely all of you have had Ward Cleaver moments when you've been stellar parents. There are other times when you've probably screwed up. That's all right. Kids are forgiving and you get lots of opportunities to try again. Can any of you remember a time when one of your parents did the less than optimal thing? See? You survived and lived to tell the tale. Most of us do the best we can at the moment. Our intentions are good, but we're not perfect. So, if you feel like it, talk about your Kodak moments and it's okay to tell us about those other times, too. I guarantee that there will be others here who will understand and have done the same thing or something like it."

Mel took a step forward. "Have you ever felt stuck in a rut? Or, you're on a treadmill, plodding along, doing the same thing but never getting anywhere?' All parents get tired at times because of their busy lives. But when your child has extra challenges, it can be even more wearying. Sometimes to just make it through the day, you fall into the pattern you've developed, whether or not that pattern is actually working for you. We all do it."

"That's part of the reason for this group," Rob explained. "What we hope to do here is to help you identify which patterns are working for you and which aren't. Then, we'll look at ways to mix it up."

A couple of people groaned. An older woman said, "Honey, my life is mixed up enough already. I don't think I could survive any more mixing."

"Bad choice of words, I guess. Sorry," Rob said. "I get that the thought of turning your life upside down is unappealing and not even doable. But what if you could change one thing, just one little thing that would make your life easier - make your world flow just a little bit more smoothly?" He let those words sink in.

Mel told them, "I guarantee that we can do this. All your problems will not go away, but if we work together, we can each pick one small area where we'll make some changes that will help both you and your child. Guaranteed."

"Yeah, how can you guarantee that?" someone called out.

"There are no written guarantees. Of course not. And we can't do it for you or for your family. But we do know some tricks - simple things that have worked for other families and will likely help yours. Look, wouldn't life be better if just one chronic hassle was gone? Or lessened? That can happen."

"And then when it does, and you get that new habit firmly in place, you can move on to the next issue that's really bugging you and make some improvements there. It will snowball until you find your life is getting easier and your child is calmer and more confident. That will give your whole family the courage to venture out and try more new things. The more successful experiences you get under your belt, the better you'll feel and the more you can tackle," Rob added. "So, at coffee, did any of you find a common theme, some problem you share that you'd like to work on?"

One father raised his hand and said, "My wife and I would love to be able to go out for dinner as a family. It doesn't have to someplace fancy, even just a pizza joint would be fine."

Mel asked, "How many of you feel this is a problem in your family as well?" Hands went up all over but one woman said, "After the last time we tried, who would want to? We all ended up so mad at each other that I cringe every time I drive by that restaurant." Laughter came from various quarters. They could relate.

"Okay," Mel continued. "That's one thing we can work on. First though, how many of you have kids on the autism spectrum, or whom you suspect might have some of the characteristics of autism?" When a few people hesitated, she added, "It doesn't matter if they have an official diagnosis or even if that word, autism, scares you off. I'm looking more for characteristics here than an exact label." Almost everyone in the room raised their hand.

One couple said, "We had thought our daughter might have autism or Asperger's, but instead her diagnosis came back as Nonverbal Learning Disability."

Mel nodded then turned to the woman who had introduced herself as a foster mother. "You mentioned that you have three boys who have fetal alcohol syndrome. Is that right?"

The woman agreed.

"Close enough. We can use the same...."

She was interrupted by one mother. "What do you mean, 'Close enough'?" My Jack has autism, not FAS. You just finished telling us that it is not our fault. Well, I for one did not drink while I was pregnant, so I did not give my son his problems. I resent you lumping me in with someone who did actual, intentional harm to their baby." She crossed her arms over her chest.

Mel replied. "I said close enough because both autism spectrum disorders and fetal alcohol spectrum disorders have a neurological basis. They share many characteristics and pretty much the same strategies work with both groups.

"And yes, FAS is caused by fetal exposure to alcohol prenatally. And yes, that is a preventable condition. But I think it would be an extremely rare mother-to-be who gets up in the morning saying to herself, 'Today I think I'll harm my baby.' Some mothers drink before they even realize they are pregnant. Those with erratic menstrual cycles may not know for months that they are expecting and by then the damage may have been done.

"For our purposes, we're not looking into the causes or even the prevention right now. We're going to look at clusters of symptoms and how best to respond to them and the strategies that will likely help." She turned to the mom of the girl with a Nonverbal Learning Disability. "And, we can use some of the same strategies for kids with NVLD as well. You'll just have to remember not to rely on visual representations, but to use words, since NVLD kids are strong in the language area."

Before Mel could continue, one father stood and called out, "You know lady, I resent having to tiptoe around my kid. This wasn't what I bargained for. Before we had Zeke, we said that any kid would fit into our lifestyle. We weren't changing; we would fit the baby into our household. I still stand by that. I'm the adult. I support this family, and I make the decisions. I resent that a kid who has not even reached puberty seems to run our lives." There were murmurs of assent around the room.

"I don't blame you. You're totally right that you're the adult and you're the one in charge. Does it feel that way most days though?"

"Hell, no," was the answer. "No! This kid has us by the short hairs and we're tiptoeing around, trying not to upset the apple cart because when it goes over, look out. We all suffer and it can go on and on and on. Just to have some peace, we give in and cater to the little bugger. Look, don't get me wrong. I love my son; he means the world to me. But he's running our lives, ruining our lives. And on top of it all, he doesn't seem happy either. We're about at the end of our rope."

"Isn't it strange," Mel said, "How a child can frustrate you so much, yet you love him so much? I think everyone here shares the same feelings you expressed from time to time. They just might not put those feelings into words as well as you did. Thank you. You've raised some key points."

Rob's turn. "That's a big part of why we started this group. We heard over and over how frustrated loving, well-meaning parents were. And, how frightened they were that their kids were not getting easier to live with but more difficult. We don't have all the answers, that's for sure. But what we do provide is a forum to talk about what's working for you, what isn't and gather ideas for you to try. We also try to help by breaking these strategies into useable parts, things you can actually do in the average home without requiring the services of a team of professionals or a boat load of money." He addressed the disgruntled father. "Is going to a restaurant a problem for your family?"

"It's gotta be at least two years since we last tried it. The whole experience was such a disaster that we just gave up. It's not worth the aggravation and time and wasted money. Not to mention the embarrassment. God, it was awful."

"What happened?"

"Well, we made a reservation. It wasn't exactly a posh place we were going to, just one of the better chains of pizza and pasta places. The reservation was an attempt to make sure we that we didn't have to stand in line. We anticipated that would ruin the evening before it had hardly begun."

"That was good thinking."

"Yeah, well, we patted ourselves on the back too soon. To get to our table, the waitress took us by this water fall. To some people that might have been a nice addition to the ambience, but it was the start of everything coming apart for us. Zeke wanted to stop and look. That wasn't a big deal; I'm sure many kids want to take a closer look. Hell, I did too. But looking wasn't enough. Zeke wanted to trail his fingers in the water. He has this thing about water, you know. When the waitress noticed we weren't following her, she turned around and saw what Zeke was doing. She told him to get his hands out of the water that it wasn't allowed and was bad for the fish. Until then Zeke hadn't noticed the fish in the water. I guess they avoided his fingers and just swam the other way. These were gorgeous fish, some of the biggest carp I've ever seen. The way the overhead lights struck them, they gleamed golden in the water." He sighed. "Zeke has always loved shiny things. My wife and I looked at each other and knew we were in for a hurdle. I tried to distract him with a light touch to his shoulder and a reminder that our table was ready. He ignored me. I could feel my wife's tension and when she's like that, her voice gets all funny. She got behind Zeke and tried to herd him in the direction of the table and I got in between Zeke and the water. He resisted. I mean he just planted his feet on the floor and wouldn't move. If my wife hadn't stopped, she would have bowled him over.

"By this time other customers were watching. If we'd been at home, I'd have picked my kid up and plunked him where I wanted him to be, the hell with his screams. But there were a lot of people around, I didn't want to disturb the whole restaurant and I really wanted to enjoy a nice meal with my family. For once.

"The waitress came back carrying this little treasure box with a shiny, golden lid. She held it out to Zeke and thank goodness, it snagged his attention. He followed her to the table. Inside were crayons, plastic fish, a little book of mazes and other kid stuff. Plus, the table cloth was torn from a roll of newsprint paper so he could draw on it. Thank god.

"My wife and I were pretty pleased with ourselves. We'd handled the incident quite well, we thought so we settled down to read the menus. This place was a tad more upscale than the usual pizza we had delivered to the house, so they called things by classier names. It wasn't easy to ask Zeke what he wanted because of the unfamiliar descriptions. What seven year old knows what Catalonia sauce means? Hell, I don't know what that is."

"So, I tried to explain the choices on the kids' menu to him but even they were written in these flowery descriptions. I tried interpreting as best I could but it was obvious he wasn't getting it. So I said, 'I'll order you a pizza, bud.' He eats pizza all the time." He stopped and glanced over at Mel, who nodded encouragement for him to continue.

"Then, we waited. And we waited. My stomach was growling and I could tell by how restless Zeke was that he must be hungry as well. Or bored. We hailed the waitress to ask if she could hurry up our food. We'd already been sitting here almost twenty minutes. How long could you expect a kid to be good? Plus, the place was starting to fill up, so the noise level was rising until it was getting on even my nerves. And, the louder the conversations got, the more they cranked up the music. We almost had to shout to be heard."

"Then our food arrived. When she put Zeke's plate in front of him he reared back and stared at it. Can't say I blamed him - it didn't resemble any pizza we'd ever had before. The sauce on it was white, not red the way pizzas should be. And, there were bits of green all over it. I don't mean flakes of oregano or basil or stuff like that, but big, honkin' chunks of green that may have been spinach. Whatever it was, I gotta say it looked slimy. Zeke braced his hands against the table to push himself away from the offensive plate. His chair scooted back, caught on a metal divider bar on the floor and flipped over backward. The thunk was so loud everyone in the restaurant stopped talking. People were craning their necks to see what had happened. We picked Zeke up; he was fine - a bit shaken, but fine. That kid has good reflexes and hardly ever hurts himself when he falls. So, we finish checking for broken bones and get him back into his chair. A waiter walking by, trying to be helpful, I think, pushes Zeke's chair into the table, trapping the kid between his chair back and that damn pizza. You should have seen the look of horror on his face. My wife puts a hand on his leg to try to calm him but before she can get out a word, the waitress is back with this foot and a half long pepper mill.

"'Pepper?' she asks. Then before either of us can answer, she starts grinding away on our plates. I tell ya, someone needed to take a little WD-40 to that thing. The noise it made as it grated! And, she peppered my son's plate, without even asking. While Zeke hates green stuff, and slimy stuff, he absolutely detests black flecks on his food. That was the last straw and he let loose. God, his screams." He shook his head and looked up. Around him were sympathetic faces, some nodded, some grimacing in remembrance of similar experiences they'd had.

"What could I do?" he asked the group. "I slung my howling kid over my shoulder and headed out as fast as I could, threading my way through the people lined up waiting for a table. My wife gathered our jackets and trotted behind. We didn't even stop to stuff Zeke into his coat, but just ran for the car." He paused a few moments. "And that is the last time we ever tried eating out."

Chapter 19

Mel organized the group. "In a minute, we'll break into three groups. If you came with someone, you might consider joining different groups so you can hear more ideas then compare them later. On the table at the side are pads of chart paper and markers."

She grinned at them. "We're teachers, after all, so what do you expect? We'll use Zeke's experiences as an example since what his dad described hit an accord with so many of us. What I'd like you to do is draw two vertical lines on the paper, creating three columns. Under the first column, jot down what Zeke did - the way an objective witness might have observed him at the restaurant. In the middle column make notes about what you think might have been behind the behaviors - why he reacted in the ways that he did. And, in the last column write suggestions for strategies that might help prevent things like this from happening again. Rob and I will be the note taker for two of the groups. Ellie, would you do the honors for the third, please? Ellie, raise your hand so people know who you are. All right. Grab a chair and form groups over here, here and here." Mel pointed to corners of the room as she spoke.

Rob was at her side instantly. "Ellie?" he asked. "Is that wise? I'm sure one of the parents could do it."

Mel raised an eyebrow at him. "What's wrong with Ellie doing it?"

"Isn't she a bit too, too..."

"A bit too what?"

"Oh, never mind. I suppose it'll be okay."

Rob called the group back to order. "Let's take a look at what you came up with in your first column. Describe what happened."

As each group read out their ideas, Rob wrote them on the board.
"He played in the water."
"He wanted to keep playing."
"He wanted to watch the fish rather than sit at a table."
"But, he did follow and go to their table."
"He probably got anxious when he couldn't understand the menu options his father was trying to explain."
"He didn't like the look or the smell of the food when it came and tried to back away from it."
"He pushed his chair too hard and it toppled over, taking him with it."
"He eventually started screaming.

Rob asked, "What do you think was going on in Zeke's mind?"
The answers came from all directions as the parents got into the discussion. "He didn't know what to expect."
"Maybe he had thought supper would be like it usually is, at home."
"My kid doesn't react well to surprises, either."
"He got stuck on the fish"
"Water probably calms him or he likes the way it feels."
"He was hungry."
"He was eating later than he was used to."
"The food was strange."
"It might have been too loud for him in the restaurant."
"Did he dress up in uncomfortable clothes?"
"Lots of kids don't like fancy foods."
"Falling off his chair must have upset him."
"I'm with Zeke. A pizza is supposed to look like a pizza. I can't think of anything green that belongs on any pizza I'd eat."
"I can picture this kid, getting hungrier by the minute. He's in strange surroundings and it's getting louder and louder. But, he's hanging on to the promise that he's getting pizza. He likes pizza, then this strange stuff is set in front of him."
"My wife sneezes every time someone waves a peppermill in front of her. You can really smell the pepper from one of those things. I can see that any kid wouldn't like black flecks on his food."
Rob stood back to look at what they'd written. "You know, this is almost like being a detective. You have to try to ferret out what might be going on before you can decide on possible solutions. You've described what happened, then you've come up with some ideas as to what might have been behind the behaviors.
"From a parent point of view, what was the most undesirable thing that Zeke did that evening?"
One woman said, "Screamed in the restaurant. That's always our

greatest fear that our kid will start screaming in public. It's happened many a time. That's our worst nightmare."

Someone else offered, "He fell off the chair but that's not that big a deal. He's probably not the first child to overturn a chair and he wasn't hurt. It doesn't sound like he made a big fuss about it. Right?" she asked Zeke's dad.

"Right. That was the least of our problems," he agreed.

Mel said, "Now, let's look at strategies we could use so the next trip to the restaurant will be more successful. So, what did you come up with?"

"Choose a different restaurant."

"Pick one without a waterfall if your kid is fascinated with water."

"Or fish."

"Go early, before it gets crowded. You might get your food faster that way and it might not be so noisy if fewer people are there."

"Plus, if there's a scene, you'll be embarrassed in front of less people." Chuckles followed this comment.

"Tell the waitress that your son is hates the smell of pepper before she brings the food."

"Tell the waitress that your son has autism or special needs or something like that, but tell her quietly, not in front of the kid."

"Ask to be seated in a quiet area, away from traffic and distractions."

"Sometimes a booth is better for that than a table in the middle of the room."

"Bring along something he likes to play with, something quiet."

"Yeah, like a favorite toy or something that comforts him."

"My kid is always calmer in a strange place if we place this lap weight on his legs."

"Some kids like the feeling of deep pressure when they're anxious. So if you're in a booth, you could sort of squish him in between you and the corner of the booth."

"Or pile all your jackets on top of him if it's winter and you have heavy coats." Then she added, "I don't mean bury him totally, just from his shoulders down. Geez, don't look at me that way. Or, better yet, if things get rough you can bury your own head in the coats. I've often felt like doing that."

"Good," Mel said. "Great suggestions, although I've never tried the one about burying my face in my coat. I'll keep that one in mind. Rob, would you care to add a few more?"

"Sure. How about using a social story? On one of the earlier lists someone mentioned that Zeke didn't know what to expect. A social story would give him some of that information. Is everyone familiar with the term social story? Most of you, but not all. Okay, we'll come back to that in a minute.

"This next idea takes a bit more work on your part, but it could lead to a happier ending. Go to the restaurant on your own ahead of time. Explain to the manager what you'd like to do, then take pictures of the place. Start with an exterior shot of the door you'll enter. Then of the interior. If there are any special features, snap a shot of them as well. Then add a photograph of the table you'll sit at. But be sure to arrange it with the manager that that particular table will be reserved for you at the appointed time. You could be in for trouble if you've told your son you'll be sitting at table X but once you get there you can't have it. That would be just one extra aggravation you don't need."

"Right," agreed Mel. "And while you're there, you could ask to look at the menu so you would know which of their choices would work best for your child. Some restaurants will even let you order ahead of time, then your food will be brought to you quickly once you arrive."

A woman in the front row said, "All this restaurant business sounds good but how do you go out to eat when your kid is on a gluten-free diet?"

"Some restaurants have gluten-free items. If you spoke with the manager ahead of time, you might be able to get the okay to bring in your own pizza crust, made with ingredients from your son's allowed diet. Then ask the restaurant to add their toppings and bake it for you. If the diet you follow is gluten and casein free, bring along your own soy cheese or other cheese substitute and ask if the cook would put your pizza under his grill to melt the cheese. Then that pizza would be brought out with the other food. Your son might think he was getting a restaurant pizza just like the rest of you."

Rob paused for a moment to see how the audience was following him. Good. They were all. He worried when he talked too much, for fascinating as his words surely were, he had no doubt that he could go on and on ad nauseum. He looked to Mel to take a turn.

On cue, Mel returned to the topic Rob had alluded to earlier. "Social stories. The term 'social story' was first used by Carol Gray in the early 90s. Her social stories used pictures and/or descriptive words that would describe a social situation or a task. The story would let the child know what was going to happen, what he could expect and what would be expected of him. When the social story was about a task, it might break the overall task into smaller, more manageable steps.

"Kids with autism spectrum disorders have trouble making sense of their world. For other kids, over time they are able to make generalizations about situations and expectations. If they've seen or done something similar before, they can automatically generalize those past learnings to the new situation. They then have an idea of what to expect. But kids with autism have more trouble with this. Situations often have to be nearly identical before a child will relate the new one to something that has happened previously.

"When everything seems new and you don't know what to expect, anxiety can arise. On top of this, most kids with autism spectrum disorders also have some degree of sensory sensitivity where sounds, smells, tastes or touch can feel exaggerated and greatly aggravating."

The audience was rapt as Rob paused, then carried on.

"So, picture being flung into a new situation without any preparation. You don't know what is going to happen to you or what people will demand of you. You can feel your inner tension begin to rise. The sounds could be pressing in on you, these irritating, background noises piling one on top of each other. Then someone might touch you when you were not expecting it, startling you. A woman walks by, her heavy perfume wafting after her. The scent clouds your head until it's hard to think, let alone breathe. Then someone asks you a question. Huh? You were not paying attention because there were so many other things competing for your attention that you hardly knew where to rest your eyes. So much was going on that it was hard for anything to register. Then that adult asks you something else. You have trouble making sense of his words. What was he saying? The adult raises his voice and says it louder. The tone of his voice has changed so that you think he might be mad at you. But mad at what? You haven't done anything wrong, just trying to stand there and survive. When he asks you the third time, you know you need to respond, but how? What does he want? Then, you're in trouble. You know you're in trouble, but the noises still press in on you. The adults are looking down at you expecting something, but what? What do they want? The lights start to strobe; the sunlight flashes through the window blinds. Outside, a car horn honks. Then a hand sneaks up from behind and rubs your arm. OW! You hate to be touched like that! Your heart is racing, the panic builds, and they're all looking at you. A strange man walks up to you and no, no, no, no more. You can't take it. Your hands cover your ears to help block out the sounds, your shoulders hunch in a protective way, your face screws up into a grimace and you scream. You fall to the ground, huddle in a fetal position and scream and scream and scream.

"Does this sound familiar? Do you think this is what might have happened to Zeke? From an adult point of view, this was an inappropriate way to act in a restaurant. But from Zeke's point of view, did others behave towards him in an inappropriate fashion?"

Mel watched the group closely as Rob's words sunk in. She wanted them to get a feel for what it might be like to be Zeke, but she did not want them to dwell on it too long. For some parents, pity kicked in readily and they had trouble getting past the sadness of the fact of what it must be like to live in their child's skin. From there it was an easy step to feeling so sorry for the child that protection rather than parenting became modus operandi, doing neither the parent nor the child much good.

"I have a friend, Ellen, who is also a special education teacher. She has this saying that might sum up how Zeke felt at that restaurant. She holds up her thumb and forefinger about a half inch apart then says, "I have just one nerve left and you're getting on it." That broke the tension as the parents laughed.

Mel felt it was safe to move on now. "It's unfortunate, but we are not going to be able to change the world for our kids who have autism - not in this life time anyway. In many ways, things are foreign to them. Author and neurologist Oliver Sacks described Temple Grandin as 'an anthropologist on Mars'. That's actually the title of one of his books, an excellent one, An Anthropologist on Mars. Temple Grandin is likely the most famous person in the world with autism. She is a familiar lecturer on the subject and speaks from personal experience. Nonverbal as a young child, she was diagnosed with autism. Currently she is a professor at Colorado State University and has made a name for herself in the cattle handling industry, designing innovative, humane methods of working with livestock.

"When you read Temple's books or listen to her speak, she's clear that the world will not change for our kids. Sometimes, we may be able to get it to bend a bit, but change? No. So we must help kids with ASD acquire the skills and the tools they'll need in order to survive and hopefully flourish. That's what we want for all of our sons and daughters, right?"

Mel turned to Rob and he took over.

"So, as annoying as some of the people in the restaurant seemed to Zeke, he is in the minority. Most of us aren't crazy about being in noisy, enclosed spaces, close to other people, but we tolerate it. We do it because of the trade-off- there is something we want or something we get from being there. Is that something Zeke can learn? I think so. There is a chance that that will never become a situation of his choosing. It just isn't fun for him. But he can learn the skills to tolerate it, to hold it together for a limited, defined period of time so that he can eat a meal there with his family. Isn't that what you'd like?" he asked Zeke's father.

"Amen, brother," was the reply. The group laughed.

As they settled down, Rob made one more announcement. "Homework time, homework," amid the groans. "It's not too onerous, I promise. Two things - first, go to You Tube and watch a short video called, 'I Don't Like Meltdowns'. You'll find it at..." and he wrote on the board http://www.youtube.com/watchv=eHx8CJOZTfU&feature=related.

Next, he handed out papers that had the website link at the top, then the name Temple Grandin. "Go to Temple's website. Do an internet search on her and on her views. Go to Amazon.com, search for Temple's books and browse a few, using the Search Inside This Book feature if you don't want to purchase any of the books right now. One I'd highly recommend is called, The Unwritten Rules of Social Relationships. If you look at that book, pay special attention to page 119. There she and her fellow author Sean Barron, another adult who has autism, list the ten rules they feel anyone with autism needs to learn in order to function.

"Okay, that's it for tonight. Thanks for coming out and we'll see you next week here at the same time."

Chapter 20

When most of the parents had begun gathering their coats to leave, Mel approached Rob. Well, approached might be a mild term; attacked would be more like it.

She turned on him. "So, what was that all about my sister-in-law? What did you have against Ellie taking notes for a group?" Her expression was fierce.

Taken aback, Rob was unsure of his words. "Well, it's just a feeling. She hasn't exactly seemed stable many of the times I've met her and we do try to keep these meetings calm, while still letting people express their feelings. Having a hothead running around didn't seem like a good idea."

"Ellie, a hot head. You actually see my sister-in-law as a hothead?"

"You have to admit that's how she comes across. Remember the way she attacked me in your classroom the first time I met her? That did not seem like the behavior of a rational woman. She went off half-cocked."

"But she believed she was defending someone in need of help."

"Sure and it's noble and all that, but she didn't bother to get her facts straight before she went off on me. What if that had happened tonight?"

"Well, it didn't and it wouldn't. I know Ellie. You two have gotten off on the wrong foot."

"Do ya think?"

Just then Ellie joined them. Mel said, "Hey, there. I was surprised to see you here tonight."

"Anything to help me learn more about my favorite nephew is high on my list of things to do. Besides, I wanted to see how this guy handled himself in a group." She nudged Rob's stomach with her elbow.

Rob looked uncomfortable, the words he'd just said to Mel revolving in his mind. She wouldn't mention them to Ellie right now, would she? From the smirk she was giving him, yes, that's exactly what she was thinking. His look pleaded with her and Mel's eyes went from Rob to Ellie then back again. She seemed to take pity on him.

"I get it now." She continued to look searchingly at the two of them. "I'll trust you to look after Ellie and I'll be on my way. Far be it from me to impede the course of true love," she said as she walked away.

"What? What did she say? I don't think I caught that," said Ellie. "What was Mel talking about? Something about true love?"

"Forget it. It was probably nothing."

"I think she said something about the course of true love. She must have been referring to something about her and Ben. You should have seen them in the beginning - they couldn't stand each other, were always at each other's throats about something or other. Why would she be telling you about that?"

Good question, thought Rob and one he didn't want to think about too deeply. Surely, she couldn't be drawing a parallel between her own marriage and he and Ellie, could she? Nah, that was totally different. So, he said, "Ignore it. You know how she is."

"Actually, no. I thought I knew Mel, but I don't know what you're getting at." Ellie's face had changed from friendly into her battle-ready mode. Oh, oh. She was about to fly to the defence of yet someone else, of Mel and Mel most definitely was not in need of defence from anyone.

Sheesh. Now he was getting himself in trouble with two women within as many minutes - first Mel was annoyed with him over remarks he'd made about Ellie and now Ellie was getting ticked over something he said, or even just half said about Mel. A guy couldn't win. He'd better get out of this hole he was digging. A new topic was what he needed. "What did you think of the meeting? And thanks for your help, by the way."

"You're welcome. What's left to do?"

"Stack the chairs and put them against the back wall, gather the chart paper and markers and put them in my classroom, then turn out the lights and lock the doors. Mel had to get home right away, so I'm on clean-up duty by myself tonight."

"No, you're not by yourself. I'm here and it'll go faster with two of us."

"You don't have to do that, you know. I can handle it." Then another thought occurred to him. "How did you get here? If you'd like me to walk you to your car, I can do that before I start putting things away."

"I don't have a car?"

"You don't have a car? Who doesn't have a car?"

"Well, I do have a car, sort of."

"What's a 'sort of' car?"

"It's the kind of car you have but don't drive."

"Come again?"

"Wax in the old ears there, Sells, or is this one of those cases of weak auditory processing skills?"

"Brat. Your brothers must have been in misery putting up with you when you were growing up."

"Nah, they loved me. Who doesn't?"

Rob held up his hands and proceeded to tick of names on his fingers. "Well, there's...."

Ellie grabbed his hand and stopped him. "All right. Here's the thing about my car. I hardly need it because I walk everywhere. I live close to the bakery. The grocery store is just a couple blocks the other way. I'm leaning over a baking counter so much of the day that I like to stretch it out and go for a brisk walk whenever I can. Besides, working and eating in a bakery is enough to make one lose one's girlish figure if you're not careful to get enough exercise."

"I don't think you've lost anything." He stopped his gaze from checking her out. How uncool would that be with her standing right there watching him check her out. Yikes. Control yourself, Sells.

"So how did you get here tonight?"

"I walked."

"And how did you plan to get home? It's dark outside now."

"I planned to bum a ride from Mel. But it looks like she's gone and left me high and dry. Wait. Do you think a ride is what she meant when she said that she trusted you to look after me? I'd have called her on that but she walked away. You know, Mel knows that I walk everywhere. It's not like her to not ask if I needed a ride home. I don't know what got into her." She turned to look into Rob's eyes. "I guess I have to throw myself on your mercy now. Do you think you can put up with me?" Ellie clasped her hands together and placed them under her chin. She tilted her head to the side, smiled prettily and batted her eyelashes at him."

"Ya goof," he said.

"Maybe, but I'm an endearing goof."

"I don't know if I can argue about that or not. The verdict's still out."

"Hah! A challenge. I loooove challenges. Oh, you so should not have said that. The game's on now and you don't have a chance. You'll be groveling at my feet in no time, hoping for a crumb of my attention."

"A crumb?"

"A crumb," Ellie confirmed.

"Did anyone ever tell you that it's hard to follow your conversations?"

"No. How so?"

Rob started to roll his eyes, and then caught himself. Likely she'd have something to say about it if he did anything so juvenile. Instead, he said, "Let's get back to this car business."

"Sure, but why are you just standing here flapping your jaws? Isn't there work to be done? Or, oh, sorry. I didn't realize." Ellie apologized.

She's lost him again. "You didn't realize what?" Rob asked.

"That you're one of those guys who can't do more than one thing at a time. Like walk and chew gum, you know. Or, talk and stack chairs at the same time. It's okay, I can be patient. What did you want to talk about next, but make it snappy. There are a few dozen chairs to pile here and I need to get my beauty rest."

Rob stared at her. In college he'd taken some neuropsychology classes and wondered now about the processes at work within her skull. Her mind did not operate like that of other people. In fact, Ellie was totally unlike anyone he had ever met before. Life with her could be annoying but it sure as hell would never be dull. That is, if he could stand being around her and withstand her attacks, he reminded himself. But, right now, she looked warm and approachable.

"Earth to Rob," she reminded him. "Why are you staring at me?"

"Sorry. My mind must have drifted."

"Hmm. My company is that boring, eh? I'll have to try to do something to spice things up a bit."

"No, oh no. One thing you definitely are not is boring. And I think you've added quite enough spice to my life in the short time I've known you."

"Is that good or bad? I know. I'll choose to take it as a compliment, and then we're all good. Right?"

God, this woman. They needed to get back on track and try to have a normal conversation, if that was even possible. His mind searched for the frayed end of what they'd been discussing. Oh yeah - her car or her sort-of car. "Tell me about this car that you have or don't have."

"Okay. You'd better sit down for this."

Cripes, she meant it. She actually meant it because she stood there, hands on hips, waiting until he placed the chair he was holding back onto the floor, then with a glance to find her still waiting, he placed his butt on the seat.

"Now, hold on to your hat."

"I'm not wearing a hat."

"Geez, that's a figure or speech, Sells. Do you have to take everything so literally?"

Did she do this on purpose? Did she enjoy keeping him in a tail spin?

But, she was ready to continue now. "My car is a 1964 Gordon-Keeble."

Rob waited for the rest. She just looked expectantly at him. "Um, good. I mean is that good? You weren't even born in '66. Is the car even road worthy? Is it an antique or whatever the term is for cars? Are you trying to get someone to restore it for you?"

"Restore it for me! You ass. I restored it. I've worked on this for almost ten years. It was in lousy shape when I got it but it is impeccable now, with all original parts. You better believe they've not been easy to find."

"I admit I don't know a lot about cars, but I've never heard of Gordon whoever."

"Keeble. Gordon-Keeble. John Gordon and Jim Keeble teamed up in the early 60s in England, created a few prototypes, and then the company was sold. The new owner made a short production run, but only one hundred of these cars were ever produced. Only ninety are now in existence far less than that are running. Mine is one of these."

"I suppose congratulations are in order."

"Do you think? You obviously know nothing about cars."

"I have a car."

"I mean car cars."

"Car cars?"

She let out an exaggerated sigh. "There are cars - regular, old run of the mill cars, then there are cars - cars with special significance. Cars that are high performance, are glorious examples of an era, cars that smell of luxury and endurance. You know, car cars."

"Oh, yeah, now I remember. Car cars. Sorry. I was thinking more of a car that gets you from point A to point B."

"Mine does that, too."

"But obviously not tonight."

"No, and not most nights. A car like this is not the kind you use for casual driving."

"I'd never really categorized my driving as casual or formal."

He got a glare for that. "What I mean is this car is rare and valuable. I keep it protected in a locked garage. It's also not meant for our climate, being built in Britain. I only take it on the road in summer and never when a storm's coming."

"You mean it's not water-proof?"

"Hah, very funny. I don't want to risk anything happening to it, that's all. It's my baby."

"Can I drive it some time?" Rob asked.

"That'd be the day. And, it's right-hand drive. I don't suppose you've ever driven one of those?"

Rob shook his head, no.

"No one gets behind the wheel of my baby but me," Ellie continued. "Well, Ben did just that once but I was in a jam and really needed someone to move it for me. The ovens went down at the bakery and I couldn't get away. Ben knew he was risking his life if he'd let anything happen to her."

"Her?"

"Her," Ellie nodded. "She's a beaut."

"What do you do, just go look at it? Her, I mean."

"Sometimes." Ellie laughed at Rob's skeptical look. "Actually, I work on her - that's my hobby. There's always something to do, something to fine-tune, some swapped-out part to replace with an original. Then there's all the time I spend trying to track down parts. With only one hundred ever built, you better believe parts are rare. And expensive. That's why I don't have another car since all my money's tied up in this one."

"Why would you do that? Then you're left without a usable vehicle?"

"I love old things. I like taking something that's sad and neglected and turning it back to its original beauty. There's an online community of enthusiasts who feel like I do and we help each other sourcing parts, and things like that."

"What other old things do you like?"

"Why? Are you wondering if I'd like you?"

This woman was outrageous. Was she flirting with him? Hard to tell. But, wait. Old? Did she actually think he was old? They were probably about the same age, give or take a few years. "Old?" he asked. "Do you think I'm old?"

"Well, maybe not old old, but it's more in the way you act. You know kind of stodgy and all that."

"Stodgy!"

"Don't worry. Only sometimes. At other times you look like you might be able to have a bit of fun and I even saw you laugh at yourself a few times when we were with Jeff. So, maybe you're not that old. It's something you could work on, you know."

"Yeah, like my walking and chewing gum thing. I'll keep that in mind, thank you." With that, he got up and resumed stacking chairs.

"I guess that means our conversation is over now," Ellie observed.

"I think your parents didn't put you over their knees often enough. Or your brothers didn't pummel you enough when you were a kid. How the hell do they put up with you?"

"They love me. Most people do, you know, once they get to know me. I'm pretty easy to be around and I'm fun and I'm loyal."

"Don't have too high an opinion of yourself, do you?"

"Nope. Just an accurate one."

As Rob pushed the last of the chairs against the wall, he thought that she was probably right. She was fun. And he'd seen evidence of her loyalty in the way she leapt to the defense of friends. And with her easy manner, all kinds of people probably did love her. That made him wonder, "Are you married? Have a steady boyfriend?"

"Nope and nope and don't need one."

"What?"

"Come on, Rob. Catch up, will ya? Nope to your first question and nope, don't need one to your second question."

"Need?"

Ellie sighed. "Okay, I'll try to speak more slowly and dumb it down a bit for you. Geez, I thought that since you're just standing still and not stacking chairs that you'd be able to follow a simple conversation. But, my bad. I'll try again."

"That's okay. I think I got it. Why don't you have a boyfriend? I mean someone who looks like you..." His voice trailed off. He needed to think before letting things flow off his tongue. He did not need to give out that much information.

She flashed him a grin. "Thanks. Although you tried to pull it back in, I think you just gave me a compliment." When he opened his mouth to protest, she held up a hand in a stop motion. "Nope. Once it's out there, there's no taking it back. Besides, did you know you look cute when you blush?"

He had never felt so off balance with anyone before. He liked to think of himself as a self-possessed kind of guy, calm and unflappable in any situation. But when he was with Ellie, his world's axis tilted just a little too far. Trying to recover, he said, "Come on. Let's get these things back to my room then we can lock up and go." He gathered most of the chart paper into his arms and motioned for Ellie to grab the markers and pads of paper.

Their footsteps echoed in the silent building. There was something about a school after dark. You picture a school as teaming with life, either hundreds of little bodies laboring at their desks, or voices ringing in the halls or kids running and yelling on the playground. This silent, still, feeling didn't fit with most people's impressions of what a school was all about.

Ellie, feeling the eeriness of the place and not used to hiding her emotions, pressed up close to Rob's back as they trod down the hall. Not expecting the contact, Rob started, losing his perilous hold on some of the packets of chart paper. They fell to the floor, their sheets splaying out in all directions.

"Oh, sorry," said Ellie. "I thought you heard me coming. This place sort of gives me the creeps in the dark like this." Only the red emergency lights gave off a faint glow. She bent down to help Rob retrieve his fallen items. Their heads whacked together with a resounding clunk.

"Ow!" Rob was knocked back onto his butt. He had not been expecting Ellie's weight to bang into his. "Are you all right?" he asked as he rubbed his head.

Ellie, too, was now sitting on the floor. "Yeah, I think so. You have a hard head, you know."

"Me? I was minding my own business. I didn't expect to get a head butt from you."

"That's the thanks I get for trying to help out a klutz who drops his things."

Rob started his retort, and then remembered who he was talking to. He looked over to find her grinning at him.

"See? You're starting to lighten up a little already. I knew you had it in you," Ellie told him.

"And I suppose you're just the person to bring out my lighter side?"

"Who better?"

She had a point. He couldn't think of anyone better. Although, maybe that bump on the head had jarred his brains. But for the present minute, he couldn't think of anyone else. The world narrowed down to just her. And him.

Rob stood and held out his hand to her to help her up. He expected some resistance and anticipated pulling her weight up, but true to form, Ellie surprised him. She more sprang up than was pulled, and her momentum carried her into him. Good thing he was taller, or their heads might have cracked again. As it was, her forehead bumped into his collar bone. He had hold of her hand, so they didn't go down this time. Her face was against his chest, and to keep her there, his hand holding hers went behind him. His other arm went around her back, pressing her closer to him. Then he didn't have to hold that first hand any longer as he felt her fingers relax their grip and find their way onto the flat of his back.

For seconds, for minutes, they just stood that way. In the distance, the boiler kicked in and there was the sound of water running through the pipes. The lights were low and it felt like they were all alone, with the world far away. This felt good, Rob thought. Almost too good. Was it just him? Did she like this, too? She wasn't pulling away, which was a positive sign. He let out a breath and relaxed even more into her. Ellie responding by turning her head to the side and resting her cheek on his chest.

She felt so warm and pliable in his arms. Wait. Pliable? Ellie? There was not a pliable bone in her body, he thought. But on the other hand, this felt oh so right. Then Rob, the rational guy who always thought everything through to the last detail, did an impulsive thing. She was so close and it felt so good that he put a finger under her chin to tip up her head. Then he brought his mouth down on hers, gently, ever so gently, tentative about how this might go and how it might make him feel.

He was right to be leery because that kiss, that one kiss shook him to the core. The intensity was almost too much and he had to draw back. But, not too far back. He tucked Ellie back into his arms, his one hand pressing her head to his chest and stroked her hair. And, she let him. This spitfire was actually letting him hold her and she wasn't fighting back.

The fighting Ellie he was beginning to know how to handle, but this Ellie, this gentle one who responded to his kiss, he did not know what to make of.

What to do now? While he felt like he could go on standing here holding her all night, he knew he'd have to break apart from her at some point. What should he say to her then? Should he apologize for taking liberties? What would she do? Had that one kiss shaken her the way it had him?

Ellie lifted her head and looked into Rob's face. Her smile lit her eyes. "Wow!" she said.

Oh, hallelujah. Thank god for this outspoken, forthright woman. There was no need to wonder when you were with her. She said what she thought and you'd always know where you stood with her. His smile was gentle and his words soft. "Yeah, wow."

Ellie lifted her face to his. "I want to see if that was just a fluke," she said and she moulded her lips to his.

In a few minutes, she decided, "Nope. It wasn't a fluke."

Rob agreed. The glow of his wristwatch caught his eye as he stroked her hair. "It's late," he said. "I guess I should get you home since you have to get up so early in the morning for work." Then he hesitated, searching for the right words. There probably were none and he'd just have to take his chances with getting shot down. "May I see you again?" he asked tentatively.

"Oh, good," said Ellie.

"Good?"

"Yeah, good. That saves me from having to call and ask you out, which could have been awkward if you said no since I'll run into you at the school here."

Rob's head went back in surprise. She would have asked him out? Really? His grin was almost cocky. Her call would almost have been worth waiting for, but then, the anticipation and worry would have been too much. What if she hadn't asked him? What if some other guy took her notice?

"When?" he asked.

"Hmmm?" her reply was muffled between his shirt and his hand.

"When can I see you again?"

"How about now? I'm not going anywhere in a hurry." She raised her face again. This time the kiss was less gentle, less exploratory. She was the first to break away. "Whew. I do really need to get going. This floor looks pretty hard to spend the night on and I need to be at the bakery before five."

Chapter 21

"No!" I want the green bowl. I always have my cereal in the green one."

"But Ethan, it's in the dishwasher. This red bowl is from the same set and holds the same amount of cereal."

"No! It's not the right one."

What had started as a good day went downhill fast. When Sara reminded him that he needed to pack his bag to take to school, Ethan grinned. Then his mom started in, talking too fast and too much and acting all twitchy, like something was wrong. It made Ethan feel funny inside; he didn't like it. And then, to top it off, his favorite bowl was missing. His cereal just would not taste the same if he didn't have the right bowl.

It was Friday - a big day for the boys. After school Ethan was going home with Kyle and Mel for a play date and a sleep over, his first ever. They'd do neat stuff.

His mom packed and repacked his bag, fussing and giving so many instructions. What was supposed to be a fun time had Ethan in knots. This was not going the way it was supposed to.

Ethan checked the visual schedule on the fridge. There was a picture of his Spiderman suitcase on wheels. The photo was a picture of Ethan pulling it behind him. There was not a picture of his mom packing it, the opening it up, taking things out, putting other stuff in and messing around with his case.

"Mom!"

Sara didn't respond. She was talking to herself about what ifs and instructions for Mel.

"Mom." Still nothing. Ethan walked over to her. He took her chin in his hands and pointed her face at him. That's what she did when she wanted his attention.

Sara pulled away. "Not now, Ethan. Can't you see I'm trying to get things ready?"

Well, he'd given it his best shot. Back to the old ways.

"No! I'm not going. I'm not going and you can't make me." With a mighty shove, he threw the opened suitcase across the floor. Socks and underwear flew in a jumble. His Lego instruction book fell out and got caught under the wheel of the suitcase, tearing the cover nearly off. "No!" wailed Ethan. "It's ruined now."

Sara put her head to her hand. Oh, god. Whoever thought that this was a good idea? Okay, deep breath. Mel thought it would be all right; she trusted Mel. Ethan and Kyle played well together at the bakery and Ethan woke up excited about this sleep-over. Whatever had put him in this mood now?

Math period was over; it had been easy stuff today. Ethan and Kyle huddled around the building blocks on the carpet at the back of the room; they got to play since they'd finished their work early and afternoon recess wasn't for another five minutes.

The knock at the door caught his attention. As the door opened, Ethan stiffened. His mother was there, talking to Mr. Sells and in her hand was his Spiderman suitcase. What was she doing here? She'd ruined his morning and now was she here to wreck things again. Just when he and Kyle were having fun.

He watched as Mr. Sells and his mother turned to look at him. Mom had that look on her face again, the one where her lips were all smucked together and those gouged lines grew between her eyebrows. That face always meant bad news.

Now Mr. Sells got those lines on his face as well. They were looking at him and Kyle. Did even Mr. Sells think that a sleep-over was a bad idea? What did they know that he didn't? He'd thought it would be fun, but he was a kid. What did he know? It must be bad to make the adults look like that.

The bell rang. Ethan and Kyle gathered up the blocks and put them in their bucket. The students put on their jackets and lined up to go out for recess. Ethan followed along; his brain full of all the reasons the adults might think that sleep-overs were a bad idea.

Outside, Ethan ignored Kyle's calls to come play and wandered around the perimeter of the playground. He had a lot to think about. When the other kids in the class heard that he and Kyle were having a sleep-over, they talked about how much fun they had on sleep-overs. They seemed to think they were good things. Then, why did his mom look like that and why did

Mr. Sells look worried along with her?

Well, they were wrong. He could do this. He knew Kyle and he knew Ms. Wickens. It had to be all right. He was a big boy now.

"Ethan, Ethan." There was his mom on the playground, waving her hand at him. What did she want?

"Ethan," she called again and started towards him. She didn't have the Spiderman suitcase with her anymore. Maybe she'd put it back in the car. Maybe she was coming to tell him that he couldn't go to Kyle's after school.

Ethan backed away. In just a few steps his back hit the fence. Still, his mother kept coming and she was joined now by Mr. Sells. Were they all out to get him? Did everyone want to stop his fun? Or maybe they knew something he didn't and things could get really bad if he slept a night away from home. Maybe Kyle didn't have Spiderman sheets. What if he didn't have the right kind of pillow at his house, the kind that was funchy and you could push into the right shape?

Ethan took side steps along the fence as the adults kept coming. Then there was nothing against his back. He'd found his way to the entrance opening in the fence. He looked over his shoulder and there they were. Both his mom and Mr. Sells were coming after him from different directions.

Run! Every instinct in Ethan's body screamed, "Run!" So, he did. Running is what had worked for him for years. When things got too bad, when he couldn't take it anymore, he ran.

Ethan headed through the opening and was onto the sidewalk. A quick look over his shoulder showed that the adults were in pursuit, running flat out now. Ethan took off. There. There was an opening between the parked cars and across the road, he could see the field. If he could just get there, he would be safe.

Sara's cries changed in pitch from yelling his name to pleas of, "Get him. Somebody, please get him quick."

They were trying to get him. His mom confirmed it. Ethan spurted forward.

Rob called on every bit of strength he had to lengthen his stride. Ahead, he could see the traffic. He calculated the height of Ethan's head and knew that oncoming cars would never see him darting out from between the parked cars.

A horn blew. There was a squeal of brakes. Rob reached with everything he had and caught the back of Ethan's jacket. He threw the child in an arc toward the curb, he hoped. All at once he registered the scent of burning rubber, and briefly the sound of grinding brake pads, the howl of a child, then the thud, then nothing.

Chapter 22

The light was too much. And, what were those intrusive beeps? He just wanted to sleep. It all drifted away.

There it was again, that pressure on his fingers. Two of them felt the way they did when his hammer missed the nail and whacked his thumb. Ow! Something pressed on the one again. He moved his hand out of harm's way, but felt it tugged back again, along with that same squeeze. For the love of….

With effort, slowly Rob cracked open one eye enough to search for whatever ensnared his sore hand. Immediately, he squeezed that eye closed against the bright light. He didn't know if the pounding drums or the crashing cymbals in his brain hurt the worst. But the pressure on his sore hand didn't help deaden the crescendo.

Then a hand hit his face. Well, tapped probably, but its effects reverberated within his head. He let out a groan.

"Rob, Rob, can you hear me? Rob." There was that tapping on his cheek again. He groaned again, louder this time as something put more pressure on his hand. Warm breath brushed his face. And that scent – he knew it from somewhere and it meant something good.

He stretched his eyelids once again. Since when did that take so much effort? It must be because he was trying to do both eyes at once. There, it was sort of wavy, but surely that must be the face of Ellie. And then he was gone again.

When next he surfaced, thank god there was nothing mashing his hand. But, there was this weight on his right shoulder that had not been there before. Gingerly and oh, so slowly, he tilted his head, and then forced open his eyes to inspect his shoulder. Hair draped itself there, hair fine and silky. Rob reached up one hand to touch it. His arm felt like it weighed twice its normal weight. As he brought it into his line of sight, he saw that it was encased in a bright, purple cast. What! Maneuvering it closer into his narrowed line of vision was not easy and he clunked it into whatever was beneath that mass of hair.

The weight lifted off his shoulder. "Rob, you're awake." And, there was Ellie's face smiling down at him.

He paused just to soak in the reflection of that smile. He tried to answer it with one of his own and winced. Automatically, he brought his hand to his mouth to feel the problem, but managed to clunk himself with that cast. He noted the colour again. He turned his arm over. "What the hell?"

"You were unconscious, so I chose the color for you. I thought your kids would get a kick out of it." Ellie grinned, pleased with herself.

He decided to let that one go. For now. "Where am I?"

"In the hospital. Don't you remember?"

He mulled this over. "Not really. I remember being on the playground at school, then, well, just waking up here. With you." He looked at her some more. "What are you doing here?"

"Mel called me. After the ambulance took you away, she had her hands full with the boys and the parent. Someone needed to keep an eye on you since you seem prone to getting yourself into such trouble."

He raised one eyebrow at that. "What happened to me?"

"Don't you remember? Oh, right, the doctors said you might not." She brightened. "You're a hero. You probably saved Ethan's life. If you hadn't thrown him out of the way, he might have been killed by that truck."

"Yeah. I guess he let out quite the wail, but he wasn't hurt. Just a few scrapes and bruises."

"Jeez. I hurt a kid?"

"No, you saved his life. If you hadn't thrown him out of the way of the vehicle, who knows how badly he would have been injured. Instead, you got hurt."

"What happened?"

"I gather that you just had time to shove Ethan behind you before the truck was right there." Ellie grinned at him. "Too bad you didn't lead with your hard head, but your hip took the brunt of the impact and your head bump was only secondary."

Rob winced. "The way my head feels, there is nothing secondary about it."

"That's because you have a concussion. But I'm afraid that might pale in comparison to when you start moving around."

"What do you mean?" Rob tried to raise himself up in the bed. The movement jostled his pelvis, and every joint, everyone bone, every muscle and tendon in that area howled in protest. Rob closed his eyes and willed himself back into unconsciousness.

Ellie pressed a cool cloth to his forehead. "The nurse's instructions were to ring her as soon as you were awake. They'll talk about your pain meds with you."

Not cool to whimper like a baby in front of a woman you're interested in, but Rob did it anyway. Somehow, the choice was removed from him, along with his will, then his hold on consciousness.

When he next awoke, it was better. Not great, or even good, but better. Maybe that was helped by Ellie.

"Still here?" he asked.

"Yep. It's hard to shake me once I've dug in."

"I'm more with it now. Wanna tell me about what's wrong with me?"

"Bit of a leading question, don't you think? But maybe we'll leave that until you're more of an equal sparring partner."

Rob raised an eyebrow.

"Oh, you mean your injuries. Well, to start with, you broke your arm." Ellie ticked the items off on her fingers. "Next, you smashed your right hip bone up real good. You dislocated some of the bones in your pelvis."

They both looked down at that area of his body. "Not much can be done about that," continued Ellie. "They don't cast it or anything. You'll just need to lie still until the bones start to knit. But, moving on – there's your head. The truck smashed into your hip first, sort of spinning you around. That's when your head shmucked the truck and you got a concussion. It's too bad you didn't lead with your head; it could have absorbed most of the impact then you wouldn't have all this hip and pelvis business."

Rob just looked at her.

"But, I'm assured that you'll live. You'll even walk and all that, but maybe not for a while yet."

"Anything else?"

"Nope. All your other body parts seem to be functioning as expected." She put away her perky expression and took his hand again. "Rob, you were so lucky and this could have been so much worse. We could have lost you." She blinked rapidly.

Was that moisture brimming in her eyes? "How long have I been in here?"

"Three days."

"And, how long have you been here?"

"Three days."

Chapter 23

"Sh. Wait. I need to see if he's awake first."

"But I want to see him now," a small voice wailed.

Rob recognized that whine, but not the gruffer voice that came next.

"We need to see if he wants to see you. Remember that he's here because of you."

"Jerrod, come on," said Sara. "Ethan's just a child. He didn't think that his teacher would get hurt. It's not his fault."

Jerrod just looked at her. "Still. You still say that. When are you and the kid going to learn to take responsibility for your actions? Yeah, Ethan didn't plan for this accident to happen but that's the problem. Like you said, he didn't think."

Rob signaled to Ellie to open the door and let the family in. He gingerly touched the button to slightly elevate the head of his bed, thankful that the slow speed gave him time to adjust to the pressure on his hips.

"Mr. Sells, Mr. Sells." A little body broke loose from his mom's hands and Ethan ran for the bed. He hit it with a thud and reached for Rob's arm. Rob squeezed his eyes shut and gritted his teeth against the groan of pain welling up from below his midsection to his eyebrows.

Sara jerked her son back and held him firmly against her body.

After two deep breaths in, Rob opened his eyes and pasted on a smile for Ethan. "Hey, bud. Nice to see you. What brings you here?"

"We brought you stuff." Ethan shrugged off his mother's restraints and dumped the contents of a plastic bag onto the bed. Thankfully the contents were light. "See? We made these cards for you, all the kids did." He rummaged none too gently through the stack. "Here's mine." He held it up for Rob to see, perching it just a couple inches from Rob's nose.

Rob made the appropriate comments on the six year old's art work, then raised his eyes to the man in the room. "Hi. I don't think we've met." He raised his cast to show that he couldn't shake hands.

"I'm Jerrod Fellows, this guy's dad." He nodded at his son, who was now sorting through the cards and talking to himself. "My wife and I want to offer you our thanks and apologize for the pain our son has put you through. We can't begin to express how badly we feel about this."

"Thank you for saying that, but it was an accident. I'm just relieved that I reached Ethan in time, eh bud?" He ruffled Ethan's hair. Ethan shrugged and moved a half step away.

"Ethan," his father corrected.

"No, that's all right. I know that he's not comfortable with light touches like that. I forgot." He gestured to his IV pole and the bags of fluid running through tubes into his arm. "I'm not doing my best thinking with this stuff flowing through me. On our better days, Ethan and I understand each other."

"Ethan, what do you have to say to your teacher?" There was a pause while Ethan intently studied the construction paper creations spread over the bed. "Ethan," Jerrod prodded.

A wee, small voice said, "I'm sorry."

"For?" His dad asked.

"I'm sorry for running away and making you get hurt, Mr. Sells."

"And..." Jerrod was not letting this go.

"And I won't run away any more."

Rob gave it a few seconds, then said, "Hey, bud." There was no reply, but he waited. Jerrod started to nudge his son, but Rob shook his head no. Finally, Ethan glanced toward the head of the bed.

Rob continued. "I know you're sorry, bud and that you didn't mean for this to happen. But, it did. It could have been much worse and you could have been hurt." Ethan studied the pillowcase by Rob's left ear. "Now, let's show your parents something. Remember your figure eight breathing?" Ethan nodded. "Show them how it's done."

Ethan took a big breath in, then using hand motions, drew a figure eight while he slowly let out his air. Then he did it all again. Turning to his mom, he said, "Now you do it with me."

"Oh, I don't really think...."

Ellie jumped in. "Let's all do it together."

"That was great, Ethan," Rob said. "And tell us why you would breathe like that."

"To calm myself and give me time to think when I'm upset."

"Can you tell us when would have been a good time to use this strategy?"

"Yeah, I know. Before I ran away."

"I think you'll remember next time." Ethan nodded. "But is that breathing enough to make everything better?" Rob asked.

"No. It just gives me time so that I can think."

"Think about…?" prompted his teacher.

Ethan looked into the distance and recited. "What is the problem? What are some ideas to solve it? What is my plan? Is my plan working?"

"You got it, bud."

Jerrod interrupted. "If you know all that, why didn't you use it? You could have saved us all a ton of trouble."

"Sometimes these things take practice," explained Rob. "Sounds like Ethan has a plan for next time though." He turned back to Ethan. "Are we good then, bud?" He held up his hand for a fist bump. Ethan grinned and gave a hearty bump. Then he leaned over and gave his teacher a quick hug.

Sara teared up. Jerrod muttered, "How often does he give us a hug?"

Rob changed the subject. "I've got something for you," he told Ethan.

That perked Ethan up.

Ellie brought out the social story that Mel had created for Ethan and handed it to Sara.

"Ethan, we're giving this story to your mom. You now have homework. Your homework is to read this story with your mom before you come to school every day. Then read it again when you get home from school and again before you go to bed." He paused. "How many times a day does that make?"

Ethan used his fingers but he came up with the right answer.

"Wait, there's more. Don't you think it fair that we give your mom some homework, too?"

Ethan giggled.

Ellie handed a second booklet to Sara.

Turning to the parents, Rob explained. "What we need to work on is Ethan's self-regulation – his ability to manage the size of his feelings and to know how to respond appropriately to situations. We've been working on it at school, but the concepts need to be reinforced at home. We don't want Ethan in the red zone where he blindly flees. We've made some progress and things are generally good in the classroom now, but obviously we need to do some more work." His gaze went between Jerrod to Sara and back again. "Are you willing to work with us on this?" There were nods all around.

Ellie watched with growing concern, her eyes on Rob's pallor. "Okay, enough for one day." She began stacking the students' cards into a pile. "Thanks, Ethan for bringing these for Mr. Sells. He'll look at them all later, but right now, he badly needs a nap." She escorted the family out of the hospital room, shutting the door firmly behind them.

By the time she turned around, Rob's eyes were already closed. She resumed her place by the side of his bed, propped her e-reader on the side of the bed and cradled Rob's hand in her own.

Chapter 24

They were celebrating Rob's recovery with cappuccinos and goodies at the bakery. He'd been released three days ago and ready to venture back into the world for short stints, anyway. Ellie had hardly left his side on the first two days, but she had a business to run. So Ben and Mel gave Rob a lift to the bakery where Ellie was working.

"You do realize she's a brat, don't you?" Ben reminded Rob.

"Yeah, I kind of figure that one out pretty quickly," Rob admitted. He automatically moved his abdomen out of the reach of Ellie's jabbing elbow.

"That being said, she is my sister and I've had to tolerate her all my life. I know it can be rough. But I'm warning you, if you do anything to hurt her, I'll have to kill you."

"Ben!" said Mel and Ellie together.

"Butt out," said his wife.

"You jerk," said Ellie. "Lay off the big brother act. When we were kids I was in danger of you killing me. As if I'd rely on you to protect me from anything now."

While their bantering went on, Rob had time to think. He realized that that saying about cutting off his arm before he'd hurt her was true. He could not bear the thought of Ellie ever being harmed by anything, let alone by him. He would do all within his power to protect her. Always.

Yikes! Where had that come from? He turned to look at Ellie, forgetting all about the others in the room and realized that it was true. Everything was true. He would guard this woman with his life and grow old keeping that promise. That is, if she'd let him.

ABOUT THE AUTHOR

Dr. Sharon Mitchell has worked as teacher, counselor, psychologist and consultant in schools divisions and health regions. She teaches university classes in educational psychology and educational leadership. Thousands of participants have attended her workshops and seminars. Her Master's and PhD studies focused on autism. Her passion is helping those on the autism spectrum to become as independent as possible.

Thank you for spending time with us, reading Ethan, Rob and Ellie's story. If you enjoyed this book, please go to Amazon and leave a review. Reviews are crucial to authors. Here is the link: Autism Runs Away on Amazon.

Author Dr. Sharon Mitchell loves connecting with readers. Contact her through her website at http://www.drsharonmitchell.org. There you will find information on her other books her workshop appearances and questions families and teachers often ask about kids who have autism spectrum disorders.

To join the author's Review Team to receive free, advance copies of new books, drop her a note at http://www.drsharonmitchell.org.

There's more! If you liked Autism Runs Away, you might also enjoy the other books in the series. Each focuses on a different child who has an autism spectrum disorder. Many of the same characters appear in each book.

Here's a synopsis of each book. Following that are sample chapters of each one.

OTHER BOOKS IN THE SERIES

Autism Goes to School

Autism Goes to School Workbook (coming soon)

Autism Runs Away

Autism Belongs

Autism Talks and Talks

Autism Grows Up

Autism Boxed Set (contains Autism Goes to School, Autism Runs Away and Autism Belongs)

Prequel to Autism Goes to School (coming soon)

Synopsis of Books in the School Daze Series

Autism Goes to School

We're thrilled to announce that this Amazon bestseller is also a B.R.A.G. Medallion winner!

After suddenly receiving custody of his five year old son, Ben must learn how to be a dad. The fact that he'd even fathered a child was news to him. Not only does this mean restructuring his sixty-hour workweek and becoming responsible for another human being, but also Kyle has autism.

Enter the school system and a shaky beginning. Under the guidance of a gifted teacher, Ben and Kyle take tentative steps to becoming father and son.

Teacher Melanie Nicols sees Ben as a deadbeat dad, but grudgingly comes to admire how he hangs in, determined to learn for his son's sake. Her admiration grows to more as father and son come to rely on Melanie being a part of their lives.

When parents receive the news that their child has autism, they spend countless hours researching the subject, usually at night, after an exhausting day. Teachers, when they hear that they'll have a student with an autism spectrum disorder, also try to learn as much as they can. This novel was written for such parents and teachers - an entertaining read that offers information on autism and strategies that work.

Bonus Section
At the back of the book are links and references useful to parents and teachers.

You can find Autism Goes to School FREE at these retailers:
Amazon.com
BookHip.com/ZPHDQC
iTunes
Kobo
Barnes & Noble paperback
Barnes & Noble e-book

What Are Reviewers Saying About Autism Goes to School?

- "A gem of a book"
- " A true delight - Highly, highly recommended
- Just couldn't put it down"
- "Highly informative and extremely helpful - Couldn't take my eyes off it"
- I loved this book from beginning to end - Just plain awesome
- I could feel the author's passion - What a great way to learn about autism
- "Entertains, entrances & educates: 3 for the Price of One!"
- "This wonderful book is about a Dad, Ben, meeting his autistic son Kyle for the very first time, when Mom dumps him suddenly on his doorstep, saying she can no longer take care of him. Through the eyes of Ben, we get a glimpse of both the challenges and joys of being a parent of a child who sees the world in different ways."

- "Unlike some stories that speak of autistic children, this one brings a wealth of hope and information! As we look over Ben's shoulder, we see a glimpse of the learning tools currently being used in the classroom today, and we get glimpses of things that could be helpful in the day to day life of an autistic child."

- "I appreciated this story on several levels. First I enjoyed the story of Ben discovering what it means to be a parent, especially a single parent. Second, I enjoyed watching Kyle find his own means of success in this new and upside down world. "

- "I enjoyed the glimpse into classroom life and options available today. Finally I enjoyed the quiet romance between Mel and Ben."

Autism Belongs

Manny is not like other children. He doesn't talk. He doesn't leave the house. His parents desperately try to arrange their world so that Manny does not get upset. Because, when he does, well, the aggression was getting worse. Too many times Tomas had to leave work to rescue his wife from the havoc of their son's meltdowns. At ten, Manny was becoming difficult to handle.

Passing by a bakery made all the difference. There, they met people who understand autism, along with its strengths and challenges. They learn ways to help Manny communicate and socialize and to have his needs met.

Dare they consider letting him go to school? Is there a chance that Manny actually belongs there? You bet

Meet Kyle, Ben, Mel and the other characters you read about in the Amazon bestseller Autism Goes to School and see how they've grown and progressed.

For free sample chapters of Autism Belongs, go to this link: BookHip.com/ZSCWPL

You can find Autism Belongs on Amazon at this URL: https://www.amazon.com/Autism-Belongs-School-Daze-Book-ebook/dp/B0184ZQMI6/.

Autism Talks and Talks

Karen is a grade 6 student who has Asperger's Syndrome. She is bright, vivacious and highly verbal. Too verbal. She finds certain topics fascinating, studies them in-depth and is all too willing to share her knowledge with others. She goes on and on and on, not realizing that she is boring and alienating the other kids with her endless monologues. Her protective mom tries to shield her from the world, limiting her contact with peers in case she might be bullied.

Karen would like to be social. She remains on the fringe, looking at other adolescents having fun together and wondering if she could ever be a part of the group.

Karen has potential. Her inability to read body language and her lack of knowledge in social pragmatics get in the way of interacting with others her age and having friends. Through a structured group at school, she begins to understand the give and take of conversation and to have some positive experiences with her peers.

And, can a young man with Asperger's find love?

Free sample chapters of Autism Talks and Talks are at this link: BookHip.com/FNBACG.

Autism Talks & Talks is available on Amazon at https://www.amazon.com/Autism-Talks-Book-School-Daze-ebook/dp/B01IIUZH3S.

Autism Grows Up

At twenty-one, Suzie has withdrawn from a world she finds alien and confusing. Ability is not the problem, nor is interest – many things fascinate her. But, she has Asperger's Syndrome and high anxiety. To her, the world is a harsh, scary place where she does not fit.

Suzie lives with her mother, Amanda. She spends much of her day sleeping and most of her nights on the computer. Her mom wishes Suzie would get a job, go to school or at least help out around the house. Suzie feels that her time is amply filled with the compelling world lurking within her comp.

Amanda has two full time jobs – one involves working at the office every day, the second involves looking after Suzie. Amanda wants more for Suze, but does not know how to help her move forward. When she tries putting pressure on her, Suzie suffers from paralyzing anxiety, resulting in morose withdrawal or worse, lengthy tantrums. Suzie is most content when alone in the basement with her computer. Staring at her monitor, the rest of the world falls away and she feels at home.

Amanda is torn. She met this gentleman, Jack. It would be nice to spend time with someone other than her brother and daughter but Suzie wouldn't like it and she needs her mother desperately. Amanda's brother asks uncomfortable questions like what will become of Suzie if something happens to Amanda.

Jack gently persists and Amanda glimpses what her life could be like. Suzie resents the time her mom spends with Jack and makes her mother pay for the hours not devoted to her daughter.

Then, they have a home invasion. When an intruder breaks into the house, Suzie steps up and is key in saving her mother.

For free sample chapters of Autism Grows Up, go to this link: BookHip.com/RADWLJ.

Autism Grows Up is available on Amazon at https://www.amazon.com/Autism-Grows-School-Daze-Book-ebook/dp/B01JB8QW3U .

Autism Goes to School Workbook

Readers who followed Ben and Kyle's journey in Autism Goes to School have said that they would like a guide to help them follow the strategies that Ben and Kyle try. Of course, not every strategy works for everyone. Remember that once you've met a child with autism, you have met one child with autism. While we're all unique, there is often a core cluster of characteristics that kids on the spectrum share.

The workbook looks at the things Ben did right and the mistakes he made, despite his good intentions. It looks at Kyle's responses, then guides you to consider how your child with autism might respond.

There is space to profile your son, daughter or student's strengths and the areas that pose the most challenge right now.

The guide will help you look at the sensory issues that might contribute to the difficulties and ways to help. It discusses the communicative aspect of behavior and how you can help the child better express his wants and needs in appropriate ways. A self-regulated child is a calmer, happier child.

There are examples of visuals and schedules and space to create your own. And, there is an extensive list of references that will help you guide your child to be as independent as he can be.

The Autism Goes to School Workbook will be available on Amazon in 2017.

Prequel to Autism Goes to School

Readers have asked about the lives of Jeff and Mel prior to *Autism Goes to School*. Coming in 2017 you can read their stories. Go along with Jeff to his first try at college and living away from home. Follow Mel's path as she learns more about autism spectrum disorders. Learn about the challenges as their family struggles with the balance of protecting Jeff and fostering his independence.

This prequel will be available on Amazon in 2017. Free Advanced Readers copies will be given to members of the Review Team. To join, leave a message for Dr. Mitchell at http://www.drsharonmitchell.org.

Connect with the Author

Author Dr. Sharon Mitchell loves connecting with readers. Contact her through her website at http://www.drsharonmitchell.org. There you will find information on her other books her workshop appearances and questions families and teachers often ask about kids who have autism spectrum disorders.

To join the author's Review Team to receive free, advance copies of new books, drop her a note at http://www.drsharonmitchell.org.

And, get your free copy of the award-winning, Amazon bestseller Autism Goes to School at this link: BookHip.com/ZPHDQC

www.ingramcontent.com/pod-product-compliance
Lightning Source LLC
Chambersburg PA
CBHW070059020526
44112CB00034B/1927